SWINGING
THE MANDATE

SWINGING THE MANDATE

Developing and Managing a Winning Campaign

DHEERAJ SHARMA
with NARAYAN SINGH RAO

PORTFOLIO
PENGUIN

An imprint of Penguin Random House

PORTFOLIO

USA | Canada | UK | Ireland | Australia
New Zealand | India | South Africa | China | Singapore

Portfolio is part of the Penguin Random House group of companies
whose addresses can be found at global.penguinrandomhouse.com

Published by Penguin Random House India Pvt. Ltd
4th Floor, Capital Tower 1, MG Road,
Gurugram 122 002, Haryana, India

First Published in Random Business by Penguin Random House India 2016
This edition published in Portfolio by Penguin Random House India 2019

ISBN 9788184007602

Typeset in Adobe Jenson Pro by Manipal Digital Systems, Manipal

Printed at Repro India Limited

www.penguin.co.in

This is a legitimate digitally printed version of the book and therefore might not
have certain extra finishing on the cover.

To my father, Pran Nath Sharma,
my mother, Sangeeta Sharma, my wife, Shveta Sharma,
my daughter, Lavya, and my son, Girik.

CONTENTS

1

CAMPAIGN MANAGEMENT AND ITS IMPORTANCE

Marketing Concept to Political Campaign: the 4Ps

George W. Bush is one of the most talked about political leaders in the recent times. Pew Research Center in Washington[1] surveyed 350 Americans and 600 Non-Americans, asking respondents to complete the following sentence: George W. Bush appears to be _____. The goal of this survey was to ascertain what images are commonly associated with the former US president, and after analysing the collected data, they found that a majority of the respondents closely associated George W. Bush with being a cowboy, a southerner (a person hailing from the southern part of USA) and a farmer. Yet in reality, George W. Bush's family hails from New England, a Yankee region that is commonly contrasted with the American south. He was born in New Haven, Connecticut, and lived in the north-east for the duration of his education, earning his high school diploma and master's degree in Massachusetts and his bachelor's degree in Connecticut. Why then is George W. Bush commonly perceived as a southerner?

The answer to the above quandary lies in the way his image was managed during his congressional, gubernatorial and presidential election campaigns, where he was presented as a rural countryman. He often spoke with a southern accent, publicized the fact that he lived on a ranch, used rural metaphors and did folksy things.[2] Bush's image management may be construed by many to be a deliberate attempt to project himself as a common American and, thereby, separate his image from his family's image of being affluent and intellectual Yankees. In the years preceding Bush's presidency, both his followers and critics pointed to his cowboy persona as a major reason for supporting or criticizing him,[3] evidencing the critical role of marketing and, in particular, campaign management in shaping public opinions. In the 1960s, the American Marketing Association (AMA) took the official position that 'marketing is the performance of business activities that direct the flow of goods and services from producer to consumer or user.'[4] By this definition, the AMA designated marketing as a mere business function, despite the popular argument that marketing encompasses numerous activities in a variety of disciplines and its definition should not be restricted to business management.

In his 1969[5] research article, Philip Kotler emphasized that marketing tools can also be applied to a variety of fields beyond the commercial sphere, calling for the expansion of marketing function to include non-commercial entities, such as police, churches, public schools and political campaigns. As he continued his work, Kotler went so far as to redefine the field, writing in 1972,[6] 'marketing is concerned with how transactions are created, stimulated, facilitated and valued'.

Since transactions are defined here simply as exchanges of value between two parties, this view is all encompassing and introduces an idea that we will carry forward: that marketing is not only confined to business firms, but also includes the marketing of people, places and ideas.

To achieve marketing objectives like maximizing profits, business firms use various tools to effectively target the identified segments, most often attempting to optimize and balance the 4Ps of marketing—Product, Price, Place and Promotion. From a consumer's viewpoint such marketing tools are designed to deliver customer benefits which primarily include the following 4Cs:[7]

1. Customer solution
2. Cost
3. Convenience
4. Communication

In the ambit of our discussion on political marketing, we will conceive of these 4Ps and 4Cs differently than one would from a conventional business marketing perspective. To clarify what is meant by each term in a political context, I will define them below.

1. Product: The agenda and promises conveyed by the political parties or the candidates.
2. Price: Defined in terms of the price for getting electoral support. Here the voter is the customer.
3. Place: A substantial amount of strategic effort is required to convey the pertinent and unique message to the diverse set of voters spread across the length and breadth of the country.

4. Promotion: As in the case of conventional marketing, promotion is the most visible part of political marketing and includes various activities such as rallies, advertising, billboards, door-to-door canvassing and other campaign activities.

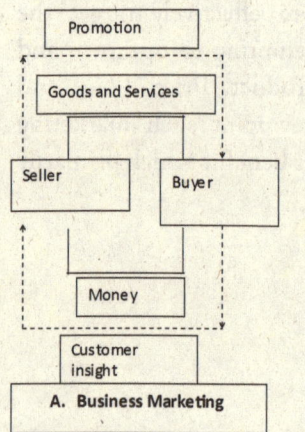
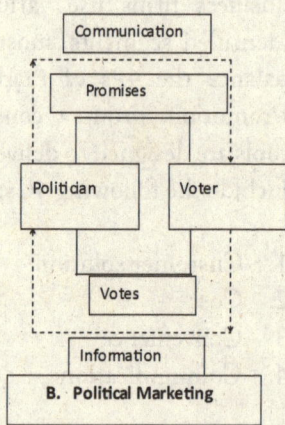

Source: Plasser, Fritz and Plasser, Gunda, *Global Political Campaigning: A Worldwide Analysis of Campaign Professionals and Their Practices*, New York: Praeger, 2002.

Political campaigning has changed a lot over the years. Previously considered merely to be the art of attracting voters by intuition and personal charm, political marketing has recently become a dynamic field. This metamorphosis from an art to partial science can be attributed to substantial growth in marketing research, growth of new dynamic digital media (most notably social media), development of big data analytics capabilities and professional agencies' increasing involvement in political marketing activities.

Campaign Management in Action: Analytical Approach and Practices

Changing Campaign Practices

In an attempt to clarify the inherent changes in political campaign practices, Blumler[8] and Kavanagh[9] have divided the development of political communication systems into three successive phases, which many democracies seem to have passed through in the last few decades.[10]

The first phase, starting after World War II (the new system became popular in the US, the UK and some other liberated countries in Europe), has been categorized as a 'Party Dominated Communication System', predominantly based on substantive messages, programmatic differences, a partisan press and group-based loyalties of voters. The second phase was media logic phase. This era of fast-paced news, improved communication and media coverage, which dawned in the 1960s, saw the advent of nationwide television as the dominant medium of political communication. In those days a new entrepreneurial profession entered the political marketplace: the political consultants, who specialized in strategic communication, image building, crafting television commercials and extensive survey research.

Currently the third phase is emerging: 'Interactive marketing phase'. It is based on our understanding of Blumler and Kavanagh's work in 1999[11]. This phase is characterized by channel and audience fragmentation, a multiplicity of news outlets, the advent of the Internet, growing professionalization of campaigns and the transformation of broadcasting into narrow-casted micro messages addressed to carefully targeted voter segments.

Dealing with changing campaign practices, Butler and Ranney (1981)[12] as well as Farell (1996), Norris (2004)[13] and Wring (2001) have proposed a model to categorize the developments in campaign practices around the world, with their styles ranging from pre- to postmodern.

Why Do People Vote in India?

For political parties to be evaluated within the frameworks of management models, we must assume that a political party can be treated as a business entity and its potential voters treated as potential customers. The profits, which are monetary in the case of a business entity, take the form of power held by the virtue of the post, irrespective of the intentions of the person. (Intention of the person here means whether position holder serves in the interest of the voters or only satisfies his personal motives.) The political climate in India has always been volatile, with loyalties shifting to suit perceptions of the voters' current needs. While all political parties claim to address the voters' needs and desires, one party will rise above the clutter and differentiate itself, winning people's confidence.

The Janata Party is one such example, becoming the first non-Congress national government in the history of the Republic of India. In the period after the former prime minister of India Indira Gandhi's Emergency imposition, the Janata Party came into power, and for the first time demonstrated a desire to tackle the issue of corruption within Indian politics. According to an article in the *Time* magazine, no government before the 1970s had made an attempt to seriously address this issue.[14] Post 2010, the exposure of major corruption scandals in India—most notably the 2G-spectrum scam, the coal block mining scam and the AgustaWestland helicopter scam—has

Evolution of Political Campaigns

	Pre-modern	Modern	Post-Modern
Predominant Era (decolonization, birth of international organization like UN, national self-determination for countries like US.)	Till 1950s	1960s to 1980s	1990 +
Campaign Organization	Local and decentralized party volunteers	Nationally coordinated with greater professionalization	Nationally coordinated but decentralized operations
Preparation	Short term, ad hoc	Long campaign	Permanent campaign
Campaign Coordination	Party leaders and leading party staff	Party campaign managers and external media, advertising and survey experts	Special party campaign units and more specialized political consultants
Mode of Political Communication System	Party dominated	Television centred	Multiple channels and multimedia
Style of Political Communication	Messages along party lines	Sound bites, image and impression management	Narrow cast targeted micro messages

(Contd.)

Evolution of Political Campaigns

	Pre-modern	Modern	Post-Modern
Media	Partisan press, posters, newspaper adverts, radio broadcasts	Television broadcasts through main evening news	Television narrow casting, targeted e-mail and social media campaigns
Campaign Events	Rallies, public meetings, tours	News management, press conferences, controlled photo ops	Professional management of events on the lines of Integrated Marketing Communication
Costs	Low	High	Spiralling up due to the involvement of more professionals
Electorate	Stable and partisan alignment	Social and partisan de-alignment	Local issue based and volatile voting behaviour

Source: Plasser, Fritz and Plasser, Gunda, *Global Political Campaigning: A Worldwide Analysis of Campaign Professionals and Their Practices*, Westport: Praeger Publishers, 2002.

contributed to the emergence of the Aam Aadmi Party (AAP), which came into prominence in 2013 and, with the support of Congress, formed the state government in Delhi. The circumstances under which Janata Party and AAP emerged suggest a relationship between perceived abuse of power by the political parties and popular demand for change.

Elections in India are a fairly complex process. Keeping in mind the Herculean task of organizing and managing fair elections across the country at all the levels, the Constitution of India, under Article 324(1), has vested in the Election Commission of India (ECI), the superintendence, direction and control of the entire process for conducting elections to Parliament and legislature of every state and to the offices of the President and the Vice President of India. Apart from the ECI, state election commissions were constituted under the Constitution Amendment Act 1992 to conduct elections to municipalities, zilla parishads, district panchayats, panchayat samities, gram panchayats, corporations and other local bodies.[15] Norio Kondo's report 'Election Studies in India'[16] studied voter turnout and votes polled to parties, concluding that the different levels of elections—constituency level, state level, national level, districts, municipalities and corporations—were interconnected. He also found that voters were visibly distinguishable by socio-economic factors such as caste, education and income. Elections in India are different not because of the scale and size but the changing perceptions of the people (voters) and issues intrinsic to the country like religion, caste, patronage to party ideology and leadership, preference and choices. This heterogeneous structure effects political parties' decision of differentiation. The basis of these differentiations then goes from bottom level (rural) to top level (assembly and parliamentary).

While most of the literature on recent changes in political campaigns, structure and high-tech models of elections using social media platforms (SMPs) is dated, a few recent studies have started to analyse how the recent expansion of technology has changed voter dynamics. These studies have tried to identify the changing influences such as the 'visibility of the party individuals' and 'communication campaigns', which political branding has made possible; for example the London School of Economics' study 'Branding in Election Campaigns'[17] discusses the importance of showcasing party ideology and individual candidate's strengths in political communications to connect with the target voter segments. Therefore, when trying to understand the behaviour of Indian voters, we must keep in mind all the classical factors that are relevant in world politics, such as party history and ideology, along with other important, varied factors in India, like caste and religion.

Voter Segmentation in Indian Elections

Elections in India are different from those in other nations on account of the numerous voter classes divided on the basis of various geographic and demographic factors. At various stages in the history of Indian politics, both new and existing political parties have taken advantage of the unique behaviours of specific voter segments to increase their respective market share and garner more votes.

Religion

The word 'secular' was added to the preamble of the Indian Constitution in 1976 in the 42nd amendment and it lead to the introduction of religion as an issue of political discourse.

The amendment was meant to enhance the strength of the government. Among the major amendments, made in the constitution by the 42nd Amendment Act, India's characterization was changed from 'Sovereign Democratic Republic' to 'Sovereign Socialist Secular Democratic Republic.'[18] In many cases, voters from different religions exhibit different voting behaviours, which political parties must understand and respond to suitably if they are to succeed. The Bharatiya Janata Party (BJP) used the 'Hindutva' agenda to increase awareness among the Hindu communities in India and garner their votes. India's minorities have repeatedly demonstrated a tendency to vote en block, based on denominational consideration rather than governance and livelihood issues.

Caste

Caste is a significant basis for differentiation in India, as is exemplified by the rise of Lalu Prasad Yadav in Bihar in the 1990s. With the unflinching support of his Yadav caste, Lalu Prasad inverted Bihar's caste pyramid, creating a new power structure that broke the stranglehold of the Brahmin–Bhumihar–Kayastha leadership. The state's 16 per cent Yadav votes were supported by 18 per cent Muslim votes, and the mixture of religion- and caste-based politics proved to be an unbeatable combination.[19]

Language

Recently, the importance of language as a basis for voting behaviour has gradually increased. In the southern part of the country, political parties such as All India Anna Dravida Munnetra Kazhagam (AIADMK) and Dravida Munnetra

Kazhagam (DMK) have used specific characteristics of language as a voter segment to increase their appeal in the states. The All India Trinamool Congress (TMC) party in West Bengal used the formula of '*Maa Mati Manush*—Mother Motherland and People' successfully to come out victorious in the 2011 assembly elections.[20] This represents a stark deviation from popular political strategies of the 1960s, when the Shiv Sena, among others, focused on appealing to voters' dissatisfaction with the current government, sidetracking the importance of language and culture. Language plays an equally important role in national politics. Usually, Prime Minister Narendra Modi's political speeches are dominated by the issues of good governance and administration, but when he speaks in his home state of Gujarat, he often focuses on Gujarati pride and language.[21]

Income Level

Another line along which Indian voting patterns are divided is that of income level. It is increasingly being observed that voters from the low-income group vote for political parties and those from the high-income group vote for candidates after looking at their performance and political agenda. Political parties have successfully leveraged these differences to increase their vote share. Additionally, issues such as 'survival' and influencing factors such as public input, relatives, friends, community leaders, schoolteachers and religious leaders are used to attract the lower-income group. Some parties create a pro-poor value proposition through gimmicks like free power, fertilizer subsidies, etc. Slum vote banks in urban areas are also commonly targeted through such tactics. For example, slums in Mumbai became a huge vote bank for Congress in the early years of the new millennium when the Congress government decided to legalize slums in Mumbai.[22]

Regional Issues

Region also significantly influences voter segments, as different regions are attracted to different value propositions. The Congress presented itself as a party with better governance and administration in Maharashtra, whereas in Gujarat their major focus has been on secularism.

Issue-Based Segmentation

Issue-based politics is another trend that has emerged in the country. Aam Aadmi Party used the issue of corruption to quickly reach the top. They achieved significant attention from the masses, particularly youth and working-class people, and in a very short time became a preferred choice for voters. In Gujarat and Bihar, the BJP successfully used the issue of development to garner political support during multiple tenures. AIADMK and DMK frequently emphasize the issue of Sri Lankan Tamils.[23] Also, the communication campaigns and marketing channels have evolved over time, and today there are multiple tools in a political marketer's hand.

Blurred Lines of Traditional Voter Segmentation in Indian Politics

The traditional ways in which voters have been segmented, as discussed above, are increasingly losing their relevance, and various studies are trying to decipher the new voting behaviour of India. Despite recent speculation that Indian voters have matured, rising above petty regional and caste-based politics to focus on development and eradication of corruption, the majority of Indians still cast votes on the lines of these same antiquated issues. In a remark highlighting this point, the former Press Council of India chairman Markandey Katju declared:

> I want to ask a question to Arvind Kejriwal, who has formed his new party [Aam Aadmi Party] recently. Which caste does your party represent? Here, in India, 90 per cent of Indians are so stupid and backward that they vote only on casteist notions. They are not interested in honesty.[24]

In a report for Harvard Academy for International and Area Studies and the department of political science, James Long expressed that, 'In India, ethnicity provides the cheapest and easiest signal from politicians to voters as ethnic identification can easily be determined by name.'[25]

Considering all of this contrary evidence, the question that we must ask is whether education and income level of the voters actually affect their voting behaviour. By analysing the data from the Election Commission of India[26] we found that educated voters are less likely to support candidates who have criminal records, have gained high net assets since the previous election and have low educational attainment, and they are more likely to vote in favour of women candidates. As reported in *Times of India*: 'Voters from the low-income group localities voted for the political party while those from the higher income group in the constituency voted for candidates and after judging their manifesto and performance.'[27]

Drivers behind a Voter's Decision

As discussed above, Indian voting patterns are highly complex and they are influenced by multiple factors. A study was conducted in 2015 by the students of a postgraduate programme at the Indian Institute of Management (IIM) Ahmedabad[28] 'to identify the drivers behind a voter's purchase decision implications for political marketing campaigns in the context of Aam Aadmi Party'. The main objectives of this study were to ascertain:

1. The reasons a voter considers while voting for a party
2. The most important attribute a voter seeks in a political party
3. Performance evaluation of the current political party on the identified parameters
4. The way in which certain people, parameters, sources of information, etc., influence the key decision-making process of the voter

Eight purchase drivers were used in the study for evaluating what is important to a voter while voting, and the respondents were asked to rank these eight purchase drivers according to their importance. The table below summarizes the responses regarding median ranks given by respondents to various purchase drivers.

Attribute	Median Rank
Party Ideology	1
Political Agenda	4
Party Leader	3

(Contd.)

Attribute	Median Rank
Constituency Candidate	4
Communication Campaign	6
Established History	6
Proven Ability	4
Direct Benefits	7

Source: Duggal, A., Chaddha, G., Yadav, H., Singh, K.O., Kulkarni, K. and Katiyar, R., 'Drivers behind a Voter's Purchase Decision and Implications for Political Marketing Campaigns', (group project report for Business Research Methods Course), Indian Institute of Management Ahmedabad, 2015.

By the median rank test, it is inferred that party ideology and party leader are the most important purchase drivers for voters. Further, factor analysis of the data shows that party attributes that drive voter's purchase decision can be broadly categorized into two sets of factors—relatively constant factors and relatively dynamic factors.

Static Purchase Drivers (Factor 1)	Dynamic Purchase Drivers (Factor 2)
Proven Ability	Political Agenda
Established History	Party Leader
Party Ideology	Communication Campaign
Constituency Candidate	Direct Benefits

Source: Duggal, A., Chaddha, G., Yadav, H., Singh, K.O., Kulkarni, K. and Katiyar, R., 'Drivers behind a Voter's Purchase Decision and Implications for Political Marketing Campaigns', (group project report for Business Research Methods Course), Indian Institute of Management Ahmedabad, 2015.

When considering static factors, it is quite intuitive that established history, proven ability and party ideology are relatively stagnant and don't change much over time. Also, a constituency candidate is actually a mingling of factors such as caste and religion of the voter himself (as we saw in language processing) and therefore is also a relatively stable factor.

In driving factors, we see attributes such as party leader, communication campaign, direct benefits and political agenda. These factors change quickly and are starkly different in each of the elections for each political party.

These insights are very helpful in bringing out a conclusion that when a political party is driving its marketing campaign, it should take cognizance of the fact that voters view both these sets of factors separately and require a unique strategy.

The study further infers that there are various purchase drivers for diverse voter segments.

1. Students: Young students are enthusiastic and easy to influence. Therefore, communication campaigns that focus on the righteousness of the party ideology are crucial drivers in their purchase decision. Besides this, they also value direct benefits that may be derived from supporting—or volunteering for—any political party. These direct benefits might be in the form of money, respect, status, etc. The best way to reach these voters is through digital media—online and social—and they are primarily influenced by friends and colleagues.

2. Working Professionals: Working professionals who were contacted for the survey were highly educated and worked in multinationals, hence they were expected to be aware of the country's current political climate. Political agenda

and party ideology proved to be their primary purchase drivers. This demographic is largely tech-savvy, so the best way to connect with them is through digital media. Their opinions are most heavily influenced by expert opinions.

3. Homemakers: Data gathered on the housewives' sources of influence suggest that they are highly driven by communication campaigns because they frequently watch television soap operas. A secondary influence proved to be family opinion, meaning that established history of a party also assumed high importance.

Overall, this study indicates that political agenda and political ideology are the key differentiating factors in the changing environment of the Indian politics. But voters cannot be captured just by focusing on dynamic factors related to elections; they also require political parties to have some static attributes (e.g. political image and history), which must be built over time. Current attempts to change the discourse of Indian polity by emerging political parties like AAP are only sustainable if these parties make a conscious effort over a period of time to build a brand that stands for something. This will also construct an image of established history for the political party. Another important finding is that caste-, religion- and region-specific issues are still relevant and cannot be ignored. All aspects of India, both modern and traditional, must be taken into account by the campaign managers of today's political parties.

Global Political Campaigns in Action

Observing the American presidential campaigns, Australian parliamentary campaigns, Brazilian or Russian presidential elections as well as the campaigns in Italy and the United Kingdom, we might conclude that the core features of campaigning have become similar in political and cultural context internationally. In the current times, political campaigns are increasingly fought and run on television and digital media, with huge political rallies and whirlwind tours becoming things of the past. Targeted campaign messages, scripted events, repeated television and radio commercials and digital media campaigns have replaced the old ways of campaigning.

The above argument makes one point very clear: modern political campaigns have become more media and television centred. Within the last few decades, political campaigns have changed drastically due to dramatic changes in media communication technologies. This change first started in the US, then spread to Australia, East Asia and Western Europe, making its way, after some time, to Eastern Europe and Latin America. It is now finally revolutionizing political communication practices in Southern Africa, Thailand and India.[29]

In fact, in the last few decades a whole new professional industry focusing on political marketing has developed in Western countries. These are the people who plan campaigns for political parties employing techniques derived from business marketing. For example, a well-known organization called the American Association of Political Consultants (AAPC), founded in 1969, has become the world's largest organization of political and public affairs professionals. This association boasts of over 1100 full-time members all over the US and other countries. In 2002, they were handling political campaign business worth more than US $5 billion per year.[30]

Growing local competition in the US has led political consultants to the newer markets of Latin America, Europe and Asia, which are already proving profitable. There is substantial evidence that US political consultants have designed electoral campaigns in other parts of the world. In fact, the Global Political Consultancy Survey data revealed that in the 1990s, 57 per cent of the revenue for the top political consultants from the US came from their overseas clients. The most profitable foreign markets for US political consultancy industry are Latin America (64 per cent worked there), Europe (90 per cent) and post-communist countries (59 per cent). The Middle East, Asia and Africa together contribute only 28 per cent to the external consultancy market for US firms, but that business is still profitable.[31]

Another globally observable phenomenon is the Americanization of political campaigns. Many political campaigns around the world have started resembling US presidential campaigns. In fact, US political campaigns are setting trends around the world in innovative political campaigning.

The most recent example of Western influence on Indian politics can be seen in the 2014 general election and the Delhi assembly election of 2015. On top of the agenda is the ever-increasing use of money power in the election campaigns. A total of $6 billion is being spent for the US presidential elections, and the numbers for Indian elections are no less astounding. According to the official figures of the Election Commission of India, the Lok Sabha elections of 2014 were the most expensive polls for Indian government, costing around Rs 1114 crore. Also, it is interesting to see that the cost of elections has been steadily rising. A deeper look at the calculations shows that the cost was Rs 17 per voter, an increase of 17.53 per cent from the 1999 Lok Sabha elections, even after a reduction of 11.26 per cent in the number of polling stations in 2004.[32] In 1999, per voter cost was Rs 14.46. Also, the 2004 election witnessed the return of the Congress-led government. The BJP was defeated after a good show in assembly elections just prior to the Lok Sabha election. As per Constitutional requirement, Lok Sabha elections must be held every five years, or whenever the Parliament is dissolved by the President of India. In that sense, the 2004 election was for the 14th Lok Sabha, what the 2009 was for the 15th Lok Sabha and the recently held 2014 was for the 16th Lok Sabha. When we compare the expenditure in Lok Sabha elections over the years, we find that in the first six elections, per elector cost was less than a rupee. However, in the subsequent years there has been an enormous spike in election expenditure.

While the Central government bears all expenditures relating to the actual conduct of elections, law and order maintenance is paid for by the respective state governments. In addition to official expenses, political parties and candidates themselves spend an enormous amount of money on campaigning and other election-related activities. Even though the government has officially increased the spending cap for the candidates from Rs 40 lakh to Rs 70 lakh, candidates are in reality spending much more money, most of which is unaccounted for, and as a result the total cost of elections is increasing multifold. The last Lok Sabha elections were the most expensive till date, costing Rs 3426 crore, which represents a 131 per cent increase in the expenses incurred in 2009 (Rs 1483 crore). It is estimated that in the 2014 general elections the total expenditure by the political parties, government, candidates, etc., was a whopping Rs 30,000 crore.[33]

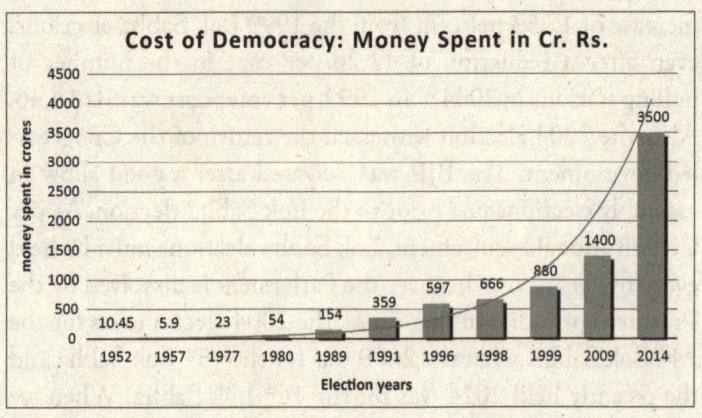

Source: *DNA*, 13 May 2014, http://www.dnaindia.com/india/report-lok-sabha-elections-2014-pegged-as-most-expensive-polls-with-government-spending-a-whopping-rs-3426-crores-1987859.

Besides exponential increases in election expenses, the increasing urbanization of Indian elections has been manifesting itself in various other ways, such as American-style fundraising dinners (as organized by Aam Aadmi Party before Delhi assembly elections of 2015), aggressive use of social media and online marketing and presidential style projection of the top candidate (e.g. the presentation of Narendra Modi as the prime-ministerial candidate of BJP in 2014 general elections, and Arvind Kejriwal and Kiran Bedi as Delhi's chief-ministerial candidates of AAP and BJP respectively in Delhi assembly elections of 2015).

Even India's news channels have become more and more Americanized, imitating Cable News Network (CNN) and Fox News. Evolution of satellite channels in India has changed the expression of political culture. As per 2014 data, there were 397 news and current affairs channels [34] present in the country. News channels adopted the unique style of open debates between party leaders; panel discussions among political, social and mass representatives; personal interviews at prime time with party leaders, termed as high-profile interviews, e.g., interviews with Narendra Modi and Rahul Gandhi (it has brought tremendous change in advertising slots for marketers), exit polls and statistical analyses, trends, predictions and 24-hour coverage of election campaigns. Furthering this Americanization of Indian politics, the members of India's grand old Congress party did something unprecedented before the general elections of 2014—they voted in a primary in their parliamentary constituencies.[35] In the US, primaries are an integral part of the political system, where party-specific voting is done to select the leader of that party. Contrastingly, the primaries are a relatively new concept in Indian politics, where certain family lineages have ruled for years. The initiative was broadly based on the US style of candidate selection. Earlier, central election committees and state election committees used to select candidates for a particular constituency. This has been advertised as a more democratic way of selection, where the grass-root worker can also contribute. The selection of candidates through primaries was pioneered by the US and has only recently been adopted by other democracies like the UK and France. Chakravarty argues that the primaries process eliminates the opacity around candidate selection.[36]

Takeaway

The above discussion makes it amply clear that elections all over the world are not only becoming increasingly expensive but also more professionally managed. As a result, there is an increasing use of sophisticated campaign-management techniques. Consequently, it has become crucial that we understand the essential tools and techniques of management in political campaign strategy.

2

CAMPAIGN MANAGEMENT: STAR CAMPAIGNER

Lately, the focus of political campaigning has changed from party-centric ideology-based propaganda to characterization of an individual as a 'product'. In a recent article that analysed the ways in which campaign management tactics have evolved over the past decade or so, many parallels were drawn between political campaigning and business marketing.[1] According to this study, Narendra Modi effectively used the 4Ps of marketing to promote his party, designing a brand-new strategy for future campaigners.

India's recent elections provide a different view of the political pundits for us to examine. The election rhetoric was more individual than the party, focusing more on the personal than the collective, and was based more on the superiority of an individual than the team. The era of one-party dominance ended after the fall of Congress and the emergence of BJP and other regional parties. In the 1999 election, BJP projected Atal Bihari Vajpayee as their leader throughout the campaign.

But BJP failed to promote L.K. Advani as their leader in the 2004 elections. During this rough time for BJP, Modi emerged as a strong regional leader. His style of leadership virtually filled the vacuum created by the absence of senior leaders. Modi, from a party worker to the chief minister, became an individual brand of development, leadership and hope. Though it may not have been planned in this way, but it has proved to be considerably applicable in the present scenario. In a sense, none of the political parties wanted to bet on one person. In the 2004 election, Congress President Sonia Gandhi denied the PM's post, a shocking decision for many Congressmen. She argued that it was against the party's ideology and practice. Here it is also referred to BJP's decision of announcing the prime-ministerial candidate before the election. Many senior party leaders were against the declaration of Modi as the PM candidate. It was perceived as too risky, due to Modi's non-secular image. In the Indian general election of 2014, individuals were turned into 'stars', who ran the entire show and eventually won the majority for their parties. This powerful 'individual personality' has been used in election campaigns in other major world democracies and has generally resulted in strong support for candidates. The above phenomenon can be observed in the US presidential elections involving John F. Kennedy, Bill Clinton and Ronald Reagan, who all swept to power riding on the appeal of their individual personalities.

The star campaigner proposition discussed in the text above finds its roots in the marketing literature on celebrity image and celebrity endorsement. To better understand the image of the star campaigner, we can refer to the concept of celebrity endorsement. Selection of a celebrity to endorse a certain product or service focuses on the personal attributes of the celebrity that enhance his or her persuasiveness. Previous research has suggested that the credibility of a source is viewed as a function of trustworthiness and expertise. The basic idea is very straightforward—generally people like and trust celebrities. Similarly, the star campaigner can be viewed as a celebrity who promotes a political ideology or political party.

A celebrity endorsement can help build trust with current and potential customers, increase the chances of the brand being remembered and attract a new type of audience. Recent research[2] has explained the aforementioned phenomenon through the idea of contagion. The theory of contagion was first proposed by French social psychologist Gustave Le Bon in 1885. In general, the term refers to anything that spreads from person to person like a disease. Later, the theory was adapted in sociology to study the transmission of ideas. Herbert G. Blumer, an American sociologist, studied this phenomenon to explain the influence of a crowd on an individual. The conclusion was that a crowd or group causes people to act in a certain way.[3] We seem to have an ingrained belief that objects can impart the 'essence' of those who have handled them or owned them before us.[4]

Celebrity endorsements have become common in recent election campaigns because the charismatic and appealing characteristics of the celebrities generate positive outcomes in elections.[5] A celebrity endorser is 'any individual who enjoys public recognition and who uses this recognition on behalf of a consumer good by appearing with it in an advertisement'.[6] The concept of celebrity endorsement has been used quite extensively in the Indian political context.[7] Celebrity endorsers are capable of influencing citizens' voting decisions in election campaigns.[8]

Traits of celebrity endorsers:

1. **Trustworthiness:** Trustworthiness is an important characteristic of a celebrity endorser as it defines him or her as a person who is credible and genuine. They must seem like someone who can be counted on and display qualities of positive thinking and respectability.

2. **Attractiveness:** The attractiveness of a celebrity endorser also positively impacts voters' opinions. A celebrity with pleasing and charismatic personality can obtain voters' attention.

3. **Expertise:** Celebrity endorsers must portray themselves as skilful, insightful, cultured and modern persons to have the maximum amount of influence on voters' attitudes.

S. No.	Traits	Political example
1	Trustworthiness	• Arvind Kejriwal started off as an anti-corruption crusader. He had the trust and support of Indians at large, which helped him move up in his political career and prove his credibility as a leader.
2	Attractiveness	• Barack Obama projected an image of honesty and positivity to US voters, which helped him gain power. • Bill Clinton was a charismatic leader with an attractive personality. • John F. Kennedy was seen as the spirit of idealism and soaring aspiration for the American people.

(Contd.)

S. No.	Traits	Political example
3	Expertise	• Narendra Modi was seen as a decisive leader with a clear development agenda that would take India forward. He had a successful development model in Gujarat which further proved his capabilities and leadership skills. • Bill Clinton had incredible people skills. He was a great communicator, with emotions, reason and character.

Table: Traits of celebrity endorsers with examples of famous political leaders.

Celebrity Endorsement Model:

The following model highlights the fact that the impact of celebrity endorsement is proportional to the twenty factors discussed in the model.[9]

Branding has become a trend in political communication. Though in the past branding manifested itself in different ways, it has recently come into limelight through the increased popularity of specific candidates from various political parties. These political party candidates campaigned strategically to attract votes and effectively positioned themselves during the pre-election promotional events to advance their external presentation. Recent election campaigns seem to focus on aesthetic and emotional aspects that justify branding. Customization and emotionalizing of politics and the way they are merging it with popular culture, both relate to political branding. Furthermore, building value, multichannel

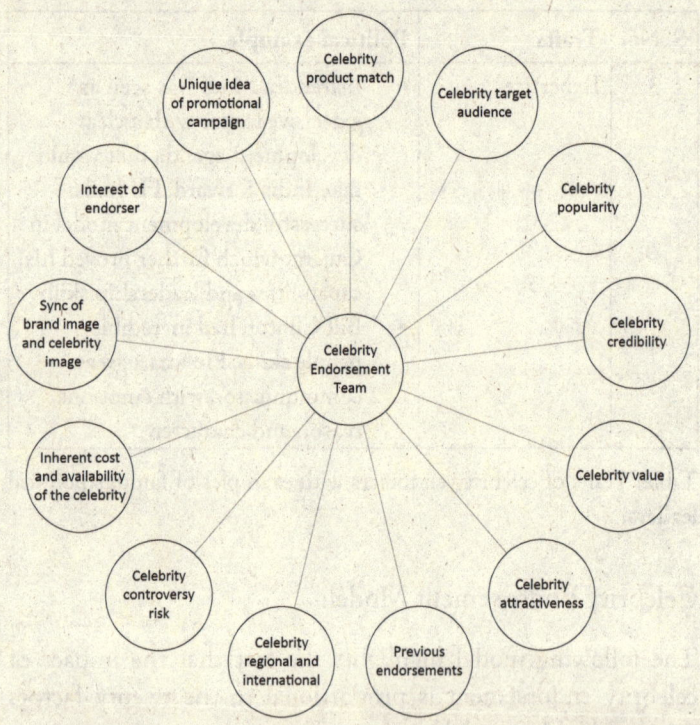

Source: Mukherjee, Debiprasad, 'The Impact of Celebrity Endorsement on Brand Image', Social Science Research Network, http://dx.doi.org/10.2139/ssrn.1444814.

orientation and trust are some of the key factors which should be taken into account when considering political branding. Building value refers to psychological representation and value-laden emotional narratives for target groups with an aim of differentiation. It can be 'functional perceptions' or 'emotional attractions'. Multichannel orientation means using different channels of communication for different sets of people, but the message and its contents are the same. Trust building is done through coherent branding and values; brands make promises that raise the expectations of consumers. So in turn, a brand must do everything within its power to deliver on the promise.

It can be hard to keep up with the ways the world is changing; politicians especially can no longer depend solely on traditional methodology and existing formulas to justify their actions and circumstances. Instead, political players now have to focus on marketing techniques, especially those related to communication, to influence voters who are experiencing a lack of sustainable political beliefs in political parties during elections. Now it has become more important to identify the star campaigner and appropriately adapt branding strategies to suit politics.[10]

Initially, the application of branding to politics seemed challenging because it had been driven traditionally, like boycotting government policies or union protests, and viewed as such by the public. It has now changed with political consumerism and market-oriented activities, e.g. buying products of those brands which follow ethical business practices or values.[11] Yet in the last few years, inclination towards consumerism has driven political parties to become more marketing oriented. Consumer behaviour in choosing commercial brands and political leaders is actually quite similar, and in both the cases the primary objective is more or less the same, i.e. 'drive the market' for a sustainable future.

In 2002, Catherine Burkitt stated, 'Political parties are the ultimate brands.'[12] A brand is defined as 'the psychological representation' of a product or an organization: it has symbolic rather than objective use value. Use value is the added value of emotional connection over and above the functional value of a product. As Margaret Scammell put it in his article, values of brands are used as differentiator between similar products. A brand can be characterized by five factors, namely cultural, social, psychological, economical and functional. In a similar manner, the concept can be applied to a star campaigner, i.e. the symbol of a political party/society wherein voters relate themselves to a leader/party.[13]

The two most important factors that determine which campaigner will be the star of their political party are strength and sustainability. Star campaigners are the 'face' of a political party and are sometimes referred to as a party's 'central brand', or the ones who are most representative of a 'distinctive brand'. They are the ones who stand out in the crowd. In both the cases, the main goal is to earn profit (votes), and the role of the chosen star campaigner, based on centrality and distinctiveness, is to ensure that the company's (political party's) brand position on a perceptual map is connected with the political outcomes.[14]

Before identifying the star campaigner for the political party, the party leaders first identify the unique nature of the political brand and the best way to highlight it. (Here, brand is associated with an individual who will play the role of the star campaigner. Again, it is crucial for political parties to make clear distinctions. These distinctions are broadly based on image, behaviour, performance, acceptability, popularity, etc.) This is a preferred approach to create a positive image based on distinctions in voters' memory. The image of brand personality is created on the basis of the individual's actions or stated intended actions. Sometimes, the influence of a political leader or brand personality is sufficient enough to attract voters, independent of the party policies. Brand personality plays a very important role in dictating voter preference, choice and intention. There are countless potential sources of political information that can impact the party's perceived brand personality.

According to an article published in the *Hindustan Times* (Patiala), 'The Election Commission of India allows a recognized state or national political party to have up to 40-star campaigners, the names of whom have to be furnished in advance.'[15]

Political parties in India can be easily compared to business companies, with their leaders or star campaigners representing the commercial brand. Consumers (voters) have a certain mindset about an organization (political party) based on its history, products and services. Also, the company has created a certain image over a period of time for a particular brand or brands (leaders) using advertising and branding in the consumers' minds. At times, it can be done either by launching a new brand or relaunching the old one, while using strengths of flagship brands.

When we talk about rigorous campaigning and personal branding, Narendra Modi is the first recent example that comes to mind. The 2014 general elections are well remembered because of the campaigning by prime-ministerial candidate Narendra Modi. He was the chief minister of Gujarat for four consecutive terms, enhancing his appeal as a star campaigner and giving the BJP a strong base to elect him as the PM candidate. Modi claimed that his project 'Vibrant Gujarat', aimed at infrastructural development and economic growth, was a success. He utilized every possible mode of communication to reach out to the people, including billboards, newspapers, radio, TV, news, social networking and microblogging; it seemed like he was everywhere, covering every nook and corner in his election rallies and campaigning.

The catchy taglines and slogans such as 'Abki Baar, Modi Sarkar [It will be Modi's government this time]', 'Congress-mukt Bharat [Congress-free India]' and 'Ache din aane wale hai [Better days are around the corner]' drew attention from every part of the country and from all age groups. The concept of 'Chai pe Charcha [Deliberation over tea]' gained much attention in the media.[16]

In 2013, according to the Indian National Election, 27 per cent of Indian citizens decided to vote for the BJP, with 19 per cent voting for Modi. Ironically, a similar percentage of people planned to vote for the Congress, and the competition seemed to be equally tough for both the parties. Yet when Modi was designated as the chief of BJP's campaign committee and one of the principal star campaigners, he drew more votes than the other leaders. This eventually increased the vote share to 31 per cent, and it is said that 'Modi won the election for BJP' as the prime-ministerial candidate in 2014 general elections.[17]

This can be compared to an advertising campaign. An advertisement has three functions to perform, first to attract the attention, second to convince the intelligence, and third to persuade, i.e. to influence the actions of as many people as possible (persuade). In the 2014 elections, Modi obtained the maximum attention (votes) with his paradoxical campaigning style.[18]

This was the first time in Indian political history when campaigning was pointedly focused on one individual. Despite the non-secular image of Modi, which was established during the Gujarat riots in 2002, he has successfully managed to engage the youth voters and to bring in a significantly large number of people in his favour. When he persuaded electors with his remarkable campaigning skills, he became a brand and later became the prime minister of the country.

The analysis of the period before the general elections of 2014 and Delhi assembly elections of 2013 and 2015 has yielded many crucial insights. Before getting into the details of the analysis, it is important to look at the background of some of the popular political figures who, despite their conservative upbringing, became the stalwarts. They were loved and adulated by millions across the globe for their charismatic personalities and appearances.

Star Campaigner in Action

US President Bill Clinton: The Most Beloved President of the US

William Jefferson Clinton or Bill Clinton became the forty-second President of USA at a very young age. Born in Arkansas to a single mother, he received the Rhodes Scholarship to study at Oxford University in the United Kingdom after he had completed his schooling. He then returned to the United States to study law at Yale University. After a brief stint as a political campaigner for George McGovern, he made his first bid for office in 1974. Although he lost the election, his campaigning allowed him the necessary exposure to win 1976's attorney general's position. He became the youngest Governor of Arkansas at the age of thirty-two. He vigorously supported education, which led to a decrease in dropout rates across the region. In his presidential role, he fought for issues relating to consumer rights and environmental law. It is also important to note that Clinton's presidential era was the longest peacetime economic expansion in the US history. Clinton is the most spectacularly gifted politician of his generation, and the years of economic boom, coinciding with his time in office, make him look all the more accomplished.[19] His political career experienced a sharp rise in 1991 when he decided to run for the presidency. The US economy was then under great strain, and the presidential elections were one of the fiercest election battles. He campaigned for a national healthcare system, a tax cut for the middle class, a reduction of the deficit and a new welfare system. With Al Gore by his side, he won the presidency in 1992.

During the US presidential campaign of 2000, the issue of US President Bill Clinton's extramarital affair was in the spotlight. Bill Clinton was accused of perjury related to his relationship with a White House intern. The scandal resulted in an attempt to impeach President Bill Clinton. Although he was not impeached, it caused much public embarrassment. In the 2000 US presidential elections, the Democratic Party fielded Vice President Al Gore as the presidential candidate. But, to Clinton's surprise, Al was unreceptive and even felt uncomfortable with Clinton's involvement in his campaign despite Clinton's credential as a star campaigner. Clinton's presidential approval ratings remain high even post the Lewinsky scandal. According to the Gallup polls, his job approval ratings reached the highest level in the year 1999—to 70 per cent. Post the sex scandal, Clinton's acceptance of his folly and expression of remorse for his actions resulted in positive attitude towards him.

Sonner and Wilcox[20] investigated the public opinion of Clinton and argue that during the time of the controversy, he was more popular than any contemporary President had ever been. The support for Clinton at the time of the controversy was attributed to the considerably stronger economy, his stand on public issues and his skills of public communication.

'Clinton embodied the optimism of the age when the US had emerged victorious from the Cold War, and the threat of

Islamic terrorism seemed remote. He was seen as a person who was deeply invested in public interest because he talked about reforms and ensured that the government took care of the public. His personality gave the impression that "he could be all the things to all people, and always managed to say the right things on most of the occasions."[21] Another important factor for his success was the peace and prosperity in the country during his tenure as the President. Despite controversies during his presidential term, as per the recent NBC/Wall Street Journal poll, Clinton is still overwhelmingly viewed in a positive light.[22]

However, in the absence of a star campaigner, the US presidential election of 2000 was a tight contest. Clinton's absence in the 2000 presidential campaigning and Al Gore's reluctance to talk about the President and the party's achievements resulted in Al Gore's defeat.

Narendra Modi 'NaMo'

Narendra Damodardas Modi successfully steered the National Democratic Alliance (NDA) to an astounding victory. He was instrumental in ensuring the party's superior performance in the Indian general elections of 2014 and was regarded as the cornerstone of BJP's success. With his hard work, sheer determination, use of technology and oratory capabilities, he has crafted the image of himself as a statesman in the eyes of the Indian population. However, he has not achieved all this name and fame easily; in fact, he had to overcome many obstacles to reach this stage.

Narendra Modi was born on 17 September 1950 in Mehsana district of Gujarat (then part of Bombay). His father, Damodar Das, sold tea at a canteen at Vadnagar railway station for over forty years. Narendra Modi was the third amongst his five siblings (four brothers and one sister). While he was still in school, Modi joined the Rashtriya Swayamsevak Sangh (RSS) cadre to serve tea and snacks to army men during the Sino-Indian War of 1962. During those days, the military trains would pass by Mehsana district while they moved from one camp to another.[23] For a period of his life, Modi spent a few years in exile and even stayed at the Sant Ram Mandir and Jagannath Mandir in Ahmedabad for a few days. He also attempted to lead the life of a sannyasi and expressed a desire to join one of the Ramakrishna Missions (Modi spent a few days at the Ramakrishna Mission headquarters in Belur, Kolkata).

Modi, a go-getter in the truest sense of the word, managed his responsibilities as a member of a political party and at the same time pursued a distance education course, eventually receiving a master's degree in political science from Delhi University. This experience laid the foundation for Modi's dynamic leadership abilities. The defining moment in Modi's nascent political career took place between 1987 and 1988 when he was assigned the position of Organizing Secretary to the BJP's Gujarat unit. This formally inducted Modi to mainstream Indian politics. Slowly but surely, Modi expanded BJP's control across the state of Gujarat. In 1990, Modi's growth trajectory inched a step ahead when he played an instrumental part in Advani's Rath Yatra (chariot march—a popular event in India) from Somnath to Ayodhya.[24] This not only added to Modi's ever-increasing political clout but also propelled BJP on to the national stage.

Modi's growing popularity within the party won him the role of the General Secretary of the Gujarat Lok Sangharsh Samiti; his primary responsibility under this new role being to coordinate with several BJP activists in Gujarat.

It was during this period that Modi authored *Sangharsh Ma Gujarat* (Gujarat's Struggle), drawing inputs from chronicles, events and personal experience.[25] In November 1995, Modi was elected as the National Secretary of BJP and he was transferred to New Delhi. As a part of this newly-acquired role, Modi was responsible for implementing BJP's strategies in the states of Himachal Pradesh and Haryana.[26] Modi's meteoric rise in the party earned him the role of General Secretary of BJP in May 1998. His strategic approach as the General Secretary of the party reaped great rewards when BJP won the 1998 elections.

Following the ill health of Keshubhai Patel, BJP's iconic leader, and the BJP's loss of power following the 2001 Bhuj earthquake, the party sought a change in leadership. Modi was the obvious choice to carry forward BJP's legacy. On 7 October 2001, Modi was appointed the chief minister of Gujarat and was entrusted with prepping the BJP for the upcoming 2002 election.[27] Modi's easy decision-making and governance impressed many, and Gujarat quickly witnessed a wave of privatization, enhancing the state's image as an attractive investment zone.

Arvind Kejriwal: Aam Aadmi Party

For the past three years, Arvind Kejriwal's name has been one of the most recognizable in India. He founded the Aam Aadmi Party and became the seventh chief minister of Delhi. He won the Ramon Magsaysay Award (Asia's Nobel Prize) in 2006 and was declared the Indian of the year by NDTV and CNN-IBN. The 2014 election surveys show that he was the second choice for prime minister after Narendra Modi. He was an RTI activist and was regarded as one of the best social activists against corruption and crony capitalism.[28]

Arvind Kejriwal was born in Bhiwani, Haryana, on 16 August 1968. He is the eldest child of his parents. He belongs to an upper-middle-class family, with both his parents having sound educational backgrounds.

Kejriwal did his schooling from Siwani and Ghaziabad and was considered an outstanding student at both schools. After seeing his zeal and commitment, Kejriwal's grandfather Mangal Chand Kejriwal wanted his grandson to be a doctor and even bought land in Hisar, Haryana, to build a hospital in which Kejriwal could practise medicine. Yet Kejriwal was more inspired by his seniors who studied at the Indian Institutes of Technology (IITs), so he decided to pursue an engineering degree there. After completing his studies in mechanical engineering from IIT Kharagpur, he joined Tata Steel. In 1992, he quit his job, cleared the Civil Services Examination and joined the Indian Revenue Service; in 2006, he resigned from his post as joint commissioner in the Income Tax Department.[29]

Kejriwal believed that officers of the revenue service, like those in the other branches of civil services, should be India's best and brightest, and he could not accept the institution's corruption after holding high ideals of service and honesty all his life. He was astounded at the acceptance of corrupt practices at the highest echelons of the Indian government. As time progressed, he gradually realized that most of the players in the system were corrupt.[30]

Arvind Kejriwal was a social activist from the very beginning. Former prime minister V.P. Singh was one of his early influences, inspiring Kejriwal with his honesty and forthrightness in the Bofors scam during his tenure as the defence minister. The real turning point in Arvind Kejriwal's life came when he met Mother Teresa at the Missionaries of

Charity in Kolkata. While at Tata Steel, he wanted to work towards various social causes alongside his job. Therefore, he requested a transfer to Tata Steel's social work department in Kolkata. However, the company denied the transfer on the grounds that he had been hired as an engineer, telling him no such opportunity existed for his position in Kolkata. He promptly resigned from his job in Jamshedpur, moving to Kolkata in the hopes of meeting Mother Teresa. After standing in a long queue, he finally met Mother Teresa and expressed his desire to work with her. According to him, it was a sacred moment when Mother Teresa kissed his hand and asked him to go and work at her Kalighat ashram.[31]

Eventually, he started an NGO named Parivartan with a few other social activists, developing a website that invited people to take part in this initiative. The first man to join him was none other than Manish Sisodia, and together they helped numerous people solve their problems with rations, electricity, pensions and corruption. They also protested in various ways against the wrongdoings of the government, extensively using banners to spread awareness about their NGO.[32]

Arvind Kejriwal: Star Campaigner in Action

During the 2012 nationwide protests against corruption, Arvind Kejriwal and his colleagues disagreed with the government on the best way to tackle this issue, and they ended up in a deadlock regarding the Jan Lokpal Bill. Anna Hazare and other members of the protesting group wanted the anti-corruption movement to be neutral and did not wish to involve themselves actively in politics. At that time, the umbrella organization of the protesting members, India Against Corruption (IAC), conducted a survey to understand

and decide on the way forward for the movement. The survey responses primarily suggested that the way to success was active involvement in politics.

Finally, Kejriwal announced the formation of a new political party on 2 October 2012. He declared that the party would be formally launched on 26 November 2012, on the anniversary of the 1949 adoption of India's Constitution.[33]

The party was launched in Delhi on the scheduled date and was called the Aam Aadmi Party, literally translating to 'the party of common people'.

The first election that AAP contested was the Delhi Legislative Assembly elections on 4 December 2013, with Arvind Kejriwal himself contesting against the Congress party's incumbent chief minister Sheila Dikshit. Despite popular scepticism, he dealt the three-time chief minister of Delhi a heavy blow, defeating her with a huge margin for the New Delhi Assembly seat. With the outside support of Congress party's seven MLAs, AAP won twenty-eight seats in the assembly elections in 2013. Arvind Kejriwal became the seventh chief minister of Delhi on 28 December 2013,[34] becoming the second-youngest person to be a chief minister of a state. During Kejriwal's tenure as the CM of Delhi, the weaker section of society received a massive relief. They did not have to run from pillar to post and pay bribes to accomplish the most minute tasks, like getting a driver's licence or procuring food from ration shops.

The AAP government promised Jan Lokpal while campaigning. Jan Lokpal was the major weapon that brought unprecedented support to the party. Party members and leaders were pushing for the legislation to get implemented. But other political rivals were not in favour of Jan Lokpal. There was a clash of interest between the state and Central governments.

At the same time, AAP declared that it was going to contest LS elections on 400 seats. Earlier, Kejriwal had said that he would not contest LS elections, but later expressed that he had changed his mind. The political drama ended with his resignation.[35]

Below is a list of Kejriwal's most important work, completed during his forty-nine-day tenure:[36]

1. Lowered the rates of electricity
2. Lowered the rates of water consumption
3. Simplified the value added tax (VAT) for the business people of Delhi
4. Played a vital role to curb corruption and inflation
5. Launched an anti-corruption helpline
6. Gave an amount of Rs 1 crore to the family members of martyred police officers

In his short stint as the CM of Delhi, Kejriwal decided to fulfil his promises to the public, even though some of them were ridiculed and rejected outright by the media. His style of governing was strongly protested. Nonetheless, the campaign style of Kejriwal appealed to voters not once but twice, giving the relatively amateur politician the top seat of the Indian Capital. His direct and humble way connects him to the people.

3

IMAGE MANAGEMENT: THEORY AND PRACTICE

The linkage of political identities and brands is not a new concept. As long as there are politicians, their branding is necessary and continues to bring in brisk business. Political parties also possess the same attributes as strong brands, like authenticity, product, purpose, meaning and the ability to live richly in people's minds.[1]

Another brand expert argues that all regions' major political parties lack focus. 'The Brand essence is becoming much diluted when the world is far more structurally complex.'[2] Regardless of whom habit favours or what leaders look like, getting your message out and making it stick does work. It is marketing 101: understand your audience, then clearly communicate what you will do for them in a way that is noticeable, emotionally compelling and leaves potent, actionable memories.

In the context of a US presidential election, all candidates develop their personal brand with the help of campaigning staff, and each created brand must make a unique statement. This is primarily necessary because politicians, just like players and celebrities, have to develop a brand strategy to promote their political agenda. They need to genuinely associate themselves with the agenda to establish rapport among supporters. This gives the brand recognition and also ensures unity within the community. It is similar to the branding of business organizations. Apple is one of the most influential brands in the world because it has focused on highlighting its 'attitude'. Similarly, people who wear Nike shoes know the brand's 'prominence and peculiarity'.

Consider Donald Trump's actions in the political arena, where he speaks his mind despite the cautionary urgings of his campaign team. That is the cornerstone of Trump's brand; he is the face of capitalism, immigration reform and the National Rifle Association. Trump wears a cap emblazoned with the slogan 'Make America Great Again', which is another part of his branding strategy. Many Indian politicians behave similarly. Narendra Modi wore the 'Modi Kurta', which became his brand during the 2014 general elections. Though the dress is traditional, normally worn only during festivals, Modi made it a style statement and successfully tarnished the age-old brand image of the Nehruvian style of dressing.

Brands are categorized as emotional and functional or a hybrid of emotional and functional, based on how they connect with customers. These connections sometimes act as the biggest differentiator between various brands. Liz Nickels and Laurie Ashcraft argue that categorizing brands in this way can also be applied to politics. To develop the relationship of this concept with politics, the authors drew a comparison between two US presidential candidates: Hillary Clinton and Donald Trump. While Hillary Clinton has emerged as a purely functional brand, Donald Trump has worked through emotional connections. The authors then highlight that the Gen Y voters, who are virtually always connected through the social media, are more interested in the emotional connection of brands.

For politicians emotions resonate and connect instantly and internally, so voters do not have to go engage in high-level thinking or sort out facts. *In other words, they understand well when they feel emotionally connected.* This emotional connection provides a firewall-like protection against any malware. A good example of the power of an emotional connection is the epic debate of the 1960s between Nixon and Kennedy. The majority of people who listened to the discussion on radio were convinced that Nixon won the debate—the reason being that radio in that time was a powerful medium. The other segment watched it on TV and believed that it was Kennedy who won it that night. The latter actually did.

Counterfactual Fallacy

The concept of contrary-to-fact hypothesis offers a poorly supported claim about what might have happened in the past or future if circumstances or conditions were different.[3] Political pundits often ask this question to themselves, wondering what might have been if history had unfolded differently. According to Tetlock and Belkin,[4] 'Although scholars sometimes scoff at applying hypothetically [*sic*] reasoning to world politics, the contributors to this volume find such counterfactual conjectures not only useful but necessary for drawing causal inferences from historical data.'

After assuming office as the chief minister of Gujarat, Narendra Modi faced the acid test of political upheaval. Issues such as the 2002 post-Godhra riots, fake encounters and his pro-Hindutva image were widely written about in the media, and these facts were presented in a negative manner. Forged letters and summons were also sent to his office in an effort to arrest him on charges of inaction during the riots. These actions and the media's presentation of the facts were intended to create a 'bad-boy' or hardliner image for Modi, but the people perceived these actions in a different (positive) manner. Consequently, Modi not only won three consecutive elections in Gujarat on his good governance and pro-business model but was also supported by voters in the general elections, and he swept the entire country by winning a majority in the 2014 general elections.

Similarly, Arvind Kejriwal was targeted on social and in print media for his unimaginable decision to quit his CM's post after only forty-nine days in office. He was labelled an 'anarchist' and considered untrustworthy. Delhi voters largely rejected him and did not listen to his explanations. However, people believed that he could bring the change required in the state, and in the 2015 assembly elections his party won the majority of seats to form the government.

These examples demonstrate the frequency of people's counterfactual thinking. There is experimental evidence available which indicates that people's thoughts about counterfactual conditions differ in important ways from their thoughts about indicative conditions.[5] David R. Mandel and Mandeep K. Dhami's 2004 study suggests that the upward counterfactual thinking differentially influences guilt and shame, independent of whether the content of such thoughts was behavioural or character logical.[6] Upward counterfactuals are the better alternatives of existing reality, albeit in thought.

'Counterfactual conditionals are those in which the antecedents are false, and which assert that one event would be, or would have been, the case if another event were, or would have been the case.'[7] Miller and Turnbull's 1990 study[8] suggests that an observer's reactions to any misfortune depend on the extent to which that event actually prompts the observer to generate counterfactual thoughts or images.

The argument could be stated as the way the world would be different if history and the consequences of previous events might have been different. This is just another way of saying that what is true might not have been true, or it could have gone differently,[9] and it can inspire people to consider alternative ways of thinking. Similar studies suggest that this way of thinking can lead people to 'false conclusions' and force people to realize 'what is possibly true, might never have been actually true'.[10]

In psychological literature, it is widely accepted that focus on the unusual, exceptional or the obvious antecedents leads to counterfactual thought.[11]

Mark Turner in 2006[12] stated that 'Mental spaces are often connected by vital conceptual relations. When mental spaces serve as inputs to a blended mental space, the vital conceptual relations between them can be 'compressed' to blended structure inside the blended mental space. In other words, 'outer-space' relations become 'inner-space' relations.'

According to Ruth M.J. Byrne,[13] people often create alternatives to reality and imagine how events might have turned out 'if only' something had been different. Byrne explores the 'fault lines' of reality, the aspects of reality that are more readily changed in imaginative thoughts. She finds that our tendencies to imagine alternatives to actions, controllable events, socially unacceptable actions, causal and enabling relations, and events that come last in a temporal sequence provide clues to the cognitive processes upon which the counterfactual imagination depends. The explanation of these processes, Byrne argues, rests on the idea that imaginative thought and rational thought have much in common.

In his 1991 research work on counterfactuals and testing hypotheses, Fearon concluded that 'scholars who have dealt with counterfactuals have often expressed apprehension, doubt and bewilderment at the sorts of logical and philosophical problems such proposition seem to require.'[14] He also questioned the legitimacy of the counterfactual proposition.[15]

Negative Campaigning

First, we will attempt to answer the common question, 'Did the media give Narendra Modi step-brotherly treatment in their coverage of the post-Godhra riots?' To answer this question, we studied almost 800 news reports from leading newspapers, magazines, online blogs, live debates and news videos, applying the partial correlation concept to each. 'Partial correlation is performed typically between two variables while controlling for third variables. Third variables might be related significantly to either or both first and second variables.'[16]

The 800 reports were then categorized and grouped based on the message they conveyed, the similarity of the news content, one medium referring to other for their content (like BBC almost always quoted news items from Indian newspapers) and the date of reporting.

After this categorization, we attempted to measure the role of media through content analysis of the 800 reports. To assess the role of media, we developed a set of parameters on which all these reports were marked. The reports were sorted on the basis of if they 'implicated Narendra Modi directly', 'implicated Narendra Modi indirectly', if there was 'neutral and factual reporting' and in answer to the questions: 'Was adequate representation sought before reaching the conclusion?', 'Were court findings accepted with grace or refuted in the name of conspiracy theory?' and 'Were the sources reliable while making these allegations?'

Then qualitative analysis of the data was done to reach a conclusion. Our study suggests that not only was the media biased in its reporting, but very often it was not comfortable in accepting the verdict of the Supreme Court monitored special investigation team (SIT). It remains to be explored if this represents planned propaganda against Narendra Modi or the insatiable TRP thrust of the media. But despite the media's unfair trial, Modi stood tall, and today he is on the verge of defining a new era for Indians.

We shall now discuss the most visible blemish on Narendra Modi's résumé—the post-Godhra communal riots. These riots have garnered media attention for several reasons. Let's look at some of the publicity and facts through an objective lens.

'Modi conspired with Jaideep Patel to instigate negative and aggressive feelings of RSS, VHP workers against Muslims,' advocate Parikh contended.[17]

This article gives the impression of factual reporting but actually covers the issue in a very one-sided way. Using strong, emotional words and an inappropriate headline, the author presented an entirely different message to the readers. A more objective headline would have been 'Zakia refuses to accept SIT verdict'.

'The Gujarat pogrom is the elephant in BJP's parlour. It is the unbreakable genetic connection between 2002 and the present that makes it clear that a Narendra Modi prime ministership would be disastrous for democratic and secular India.'[18]

This is the writer's direct judgement, even though the Supreme Court of India gave a clean chit to Narendra Modi.

The precise sequence of events; the deliberate instigation of communal violence, reminiscent of the July 1983 anti-Tamil pogrom in Sri Lanka, through allowing the display of the bodies of *kar sevaks* and their families killed brutally on the Sabarmati Express as it approached Godhra; the fuelling of hate politics and the neutralisation of the police, not by negligence but as a matter of communal statecraft and real politick at the highest levels of the State government; and the material assistance and cover provided to the organisers of the pogrom and to the frenzied mobs let loose to murder, rape, torture, loot, pillage, and intimidate so as to 'teach Muslims a lesson' and get away with it.[19]

This section uses words that are highly sensitive and implicative in nature. Moreover, the content of the article is merely rhetoric.

'Narendra Modi "allowed" Gujarat 2002 anti-Muslim riot'.[20]

By printing such headlines over a sensitive topic, the author subtly conveys that Narendra Modi was the culprit.

'However, a government report in January said the fire may have begun by accident inside the train.'[21]

This references the Banerjee committee, which was later determined to be illegal and unconstitutional and was voided by the Supreme Court of India. By terming it 'a government report', the author sends an entirely different message to the readers.

'Harvest of Hatred'[22]

This is the title of an editorial piece on the assembly election outcome published in December 2002 by a leading Indian newspaper. Narendra Modi was accused of winning by sowing seeds of hatred in the community.

'The Gujarat poll outcome, undoubtedly a setback to the fight against the Hindutva forces.'[23]

'As such, the poll verdict, which is already being gloatingly characterised by the Sangh Parivar camp as a major success of the so-called "Gujarat experiment"—distinguished as it is by the "Modi brand" of Hindutva—is not merely unfortunate but extremely ominous for the country's future as a truly secular and pluralist polity and, therefore, a matter of grave concern for the millions of people who remain committed to the liberal democratic values enshrined in the Constitution.'

'What the BJP has harvested now are verily the fruits of hate'...'Gujarat is not India and Modi is as yet only the winner of a state election'...'The BJP has won, but India should not lose'...'Gujarat endorses hate.'[24]

The above article displays a direct denial of public choice, demeaning Indian democracy. Moreover, the article directly indicts and spreads stories about Narendra Modi, shining the spotlight on him. All these comments came after Narendra Modi won the December 2002 assembly elections in Gujarat.

It is crucial to note that the Indian media was more critical than the foreign media. Foreign media usually based its conclusions and reporting on the input of and excerpts from the Indian news agencies.

'Never before has a State Government been so guilty of siding—emotionally, politically and administratively— with the rioter as happened in Ahmedabad and the rest of Gujarat.'[25]

'By any civilised political standard, Gujarat's infamous Chief Minister should have been out of power and facing criminal prosecution for his administration's complicity in what happened after Godhra.'[26]

Surprisingly, these strong and direct comments were written in editorial articles. Court proceedings and other inquiry commission reports were largely ignored in most articles that reported on the riots.

'The BJP made serious efforts, much more than other parties, to include and accommodate the OBCs so as to provide Hindutva its muscle power. He has become a bigger hero than Mr. Advani by mobilising muscle power better than Mr. Advani did in 1992. He seems to have realised that only the weapon of violence—not sacrifice—can make an individual a hero and that the social value of Dharma is assigned to the victorious, not the sufferer.'[27]

This article is completely arbitrary. It only contains rhetoric, and is based less on facts and more on ill-informed sources. These examples show that the majority of articles were written by unreliable sources with unstructured arguments. Yet this type of reporting kept Modi in the spotlight. The accusations presented by most of the media were easily handled, as the majority of them were unstructured and from unreliable sources.

As mentioned earlier, we classified all the 800 reports based on the following seven parameters:

1. Implicated Narendra Modi directly/indirectly.
2. Factual reporting.
3. Was reliable evidence cited?
4. Were adequate representations sought before reaching the conclusion?
5. Were the court findings accepted?
6. Narendra Modi projected as a nationalist, Hindu nationalist or anti-Muslim?
7. Were arguments in favour of Narendra Modi given due coverage?

Some of our most important findings were:

1. Almost 70 per cent of the articles implicated Narendra Modi on some false reports.
2. Almost 55 per cent of the reports were based on unreliable sources.
3. Forty per cent of the reports were merely a statement of opinion.
4. Almost 25 per cent of articles directly denied the court findings and went on to declare their own judgement.
5. Fifty-two per cent of the articles portrayed Narendra Modi as 'anti-Muslim'.
6. Almost no coverage was given to the arguments that were in favour of Narendra Modi.

Our analysis showed that the media, in many situations, was implicative of Narendra Modi. He is the first politician in India who has been under so much scrutiny from the media. After being tried on several fronts, he ultimately received a clean chit

The results are as follows:

Implicated Narendra Modi directly/indirectly	Factual reporting	Was reliable evidence cited?	Were court findings accepted?	Nationalist, Hindu nationalist, anti-Muslim and Narendra Modi	Was argument in favour of Narendra Modi given due coverage
Yes:119 (67.61%)	Yes:106 (60.22%)	Yes:76 (43.18%)	Yes:29 (16.5%)	Anti-Muslim:51 (51.70%)	Yes:11 (6.25%)
No:57 (32.39%)	No:69 (39.20%)	No:98 (55.68%)	No:42 (23.86%)	Hindu:5 (2.84%) Nationalist	No:96 (54.54%)
	NA:1 (0.58%)	NA:2 (1.14%)	NA:105 (59.64%)	Narendra Modi:18 (10.24%)	NA:69 (39.21%)
				NA:62 (35.22%)	

on most of the allegations, as many witnesses were found to be affiliated with political parties. Yet all of the attention Narendra Modi received actually put him in the public spotlight, which did not happen to any other politician in India during that time.

Thus we see that image impacts politics as much as it impacts other aspects of life. Many times the old adage of 'any publicity is good publicity' remains true, like in the case of PM Modi. However, politics differs from consumer brands in a few fundamental ways. In politics, events play a very important role. For example, when the former British prime minister Harold Macmillan was asked what he feared the most in politics, he simply replied, 'Events.' Events shape the image of politicians and their parties to a far greater extent than they do in business.[28]

While holding the position of a chief minister, Modi continued to respond to the majority of the allegations in a positive and assertive manner. He talked more of his positive accomplishments and continued to state that he had faith in the Indian judicial system. He even requested that he be hanged if found guilty, proudly declaring, '*Na aankh jhuka ke chalenge na aankh utha ke chalenge. Aankh mila ke chalenge* [Neither will I be subjugated nor will I be arrogant. I will walk beside you, as equals].'

On 17 August 2011, the Gujarat government eventually set up an inquiry commission. Headed by a retired Supreme Court judge, Justice M.B. Shah, the commission was tasked with probing the fifteen charges of corruption and favouritism levelled by Gujarat Congress along with other independent complainants against the then Chief Minister Narendra Modi. The inquiry commission was set up after Shaktisinh Gohil and Arjun Modhwadia of the Gujarat Congress wrote a memorandum, titled 'Details of Corruption and Malpractices in the State of Gujarat by the Chief Minister and the Other Ministers', to the President of India detailing seventeen alleged instances of corrupt practices and favouritism, two of which were not included as these instances related to matters of prejudice.[29]

The commission submitted its first report on nine out of the fifteen allegations, giving Modi and the government a clean chit. These nine allegations pertained to 'large-scale corruption' and 'favouritism' in allotment of land at 'throw-away prices' to select industrialists.[30]

Amit Shah, a close ally of Modi, had been accused in the Sohrabuddin Sheikh and Tulsiram Prajapati fake encounter case. On 28 December 2006, he was charged with organizing an encounter with Tulsiram Prajapati, a known gangster who spread terror in Rajasthan and Madhya Pradesh. Shah was also accused of organizing an encounter with Sohrabuddin Sheikh, an accomplice of Prajapati and another known gangster who had previously been charged with transporting weapons for the Dawood gang in the post-Babri riots.[31]

In the middle of November 2013, two websites, Cobrapost and Gulail.com, released tapes of Shah and IPS officer G.L. Singhal allegedly using state machinery to snoop on a Gujarati woman. The portal also alleged that Amit Shah was also involved in the surveillance. By late November, the issue had snowballed into a major controversy, and the Modi government formed a two-member inquiry commission headed by Justice (Retd) Sugynaben Bhatt and directed it to submit a report in three months.[32]

The issue was later confirmed by an official release that stated, 'The Cabinet has approved a proposal to set up a Commission of Inquiry under Commission of Inquiry Act,

1952 to look into the physical/electronic surveillance in the
states of Gujarat and Himachal Pradesh and the National
Capital Territory of Delhi, allegedly without authorization.'[33]

According to an article published on NDTV.com, the
Union cabinet's decision to approve the proposed inquiry
commission came less than ten days after the media had
highlighted that the government was considering such
a move. This suggests that the Congress party may have
attempted to use the Snoopgate case to thwart Modi's
campaign because their own election campaign appeared
weak.[34]

Despite the series of allegations against Narendra Modi
for over a decade, only one FIR has been filed against him.
This FIR was filed because he displayed his party's symbol
and delivered a political speech after casting his vote at a
polling booth at Sarkhej–Gandhinagar Highway on 30 April
2014.[35] About the incident Modi said, 'In my entire life, not
even a single FIR has been registered against me, not even
for driving a scooter on the wrong side or for illegal parking.
Suddenly today when I landed here I came to know that an
FIR has been registered against me . . . I will never forget
April 30.'[36]

Although the media largely reported the above case
in a negative light, the important thing to remember is that
Narendra Modi always remained in the news. We reviewed
news items from four major leading English dailies and three
major leading Hindi dailies from a random sample of 200 days
in the two years preceding the 2014 general elections. It was
found that, in these 200 days, news relating either directly or
indirectly to Narendra Modi was featured on the front page
at least once every week. This undoubtedly raised national
awareness of Narendra Modi.

In an interesting article titled, 'Why Arvind Kejriwal Is the Tata Nano of Indian Politics', written in the magazine *Business Insider India* soon after the general elections of 2014, Arvind Kejriwal's brand was compared with Tata Nano and was deemed one of the biggest brand failures in the country. Just as Tata Nano promised to revolutionize the Indian automobile market, Arvind Kejriwal was presented as a man who could change the political landscape. Both Nano and Kejriwal changed their battlefields, but not in the way they had expected.[37] The comparison continued, highlighting disappointment with both the brands after high initial build-up and explaining how both brands initially communicated that they were for the common people but failed to deceive and so on.

After the 2015 Delhi assembly elections, the story of Arvind Kejriwal's brand took another dramatic turn. To understand how things came to such a head after their promising start, we will look at some of the antecedents of Arvind Kejriwal's negative brand build-up. In the next chapter, we will analyse how he finally managed to turn it around.

Although, Arvind Kejriwal had been an active social worker since his student days, he shot to national prominence when he joined fellow veteran activist Anna Hazare to launch a nationwide anti-corruption movement.

Following this campaign, he was charged as follows:

1. The anarchist claim: PM Narendra Modi said, 'Have you ever seen a leader who admits that he is an anarchist and believes in the practice of anarchy? If you want to practise anarchism, then you should go to the jungle and join Naxals.'[38]
2. The 'liar': 'He [Kejriwal] is a liar. I do not know to what extent they are spreading lies about me that will remove

the roadside carts of sellers. Don't believe in him,' Kiran
Bedi said on 5 February 2015.[39]

3.   Being toxic/negative: 'His company is Toxic. I felt it to an
extent when I was with him . . . I used to have an argument
with him regarding calling press conferences and dharnas
when not needed. I think he is highly negative,' said Kiran
Bedi on 28 January 2015.

4.   Instability: 'He [Arvind Kejriwal] is hopping from one
branch to other. I am sorry, but monkeys do that.' Nupur
Sharma, Kejriwal's BJP rival, stated.[40]

In 2010, Kejriwal protested against the corruption in the
Commonwealth Games. He argued that the Central Vigilance
Commission (CVC) was powerless against the guilty and that
the Central Bureau of Investigation (CBI) was incapable of
launching an unbiased investigation of the issue. He advocated
the appointment of a public ombudsman—Lokpal—at the
Centre and Lokayuktas in states.[41]

In 2011, Kejriwal joined several other activists, including
Anna Hazare and Kiran Bedi, to form the India Against
Corruption group. The IAC demanded the enactment of the
Jan Lokpal Bill, which would result in the creation of a strong
ombudsman. The campaign evolved into the 2011 Indian
anti-corruption movement. In response to the campaign, the
government's advisory body—the National Advisory Council
(NAC)—drafted a Lokpal Bill. However, the NAC's Bill was
criticized by Kejriwal and other activists because it did not
have enough power to take action against the prime minister,
other corrupt office holders and the judiciary. The activists
also criticized the procedure for selection of the Lokpal, the
transparency clauses and the proposal to disallow the Lokpal
from taking cognizance of public grievances.

Amid continuing protests, the government formed a committee to draft a Jan Lokpal Bill. Arvind Kejriwal, among others, was a civil society representative member of this committee. Yet he alleged that the IAC activists had an odd position in the committee, and the government appointees kept ignoring their recommendations.[42] The government responded that the activists could not be allowed to blackmail the elected representatives with protests. Kejriwal countered that democratically elected representatives should not be permitted to function like dictators and demanded a public debate on the contentious issues.

The IAC activists intensified their protests, and Anna Hazare eventually organized a hunger strike. The Delhi Police arrested Kejriwal on the issue of not budging from intention of indefinite hunger holding protest at Jai Prakash Park, New Delhi. He started a debate on the power of police to detain and release people at will. He attacked the government over this issue, blaming them for using the police to advance their interests.[43] In August 2011, a settlement was finally reached between the government and the activists.

Besides the government, the Jan Lokpal movement was also criticized by some citizens as 'undemocratic' because the ombudsman had powers over elected representatives. Arundhati Roy claimed that the movement was not a people's movement, alleging that foreigners had funded it to influence Indian policymaking. She pointed out that the Ford Foundation had funded the emergent leadership category of the Ramon Magsaysay Award and donated $3,97,000 to Kejriwal's NGO Kabir.[44] Both Kejriwal and the Ford Foundation termed the allegations baseless, stating that the donations were made to support the Right to Information (RTI) campaigns. It was also highlighted that several other Indian organizations had also received grants from the Ford Foundation. Kejriwal also denied allegations that the movement was a plot against the ruling Congress by the RSS and that it was an upper-caste conspiracy against the Dalits.

By January 2012, the government backtracked on its promise to implement a strong Jan Lokpal, catalysing another series of protests from Kejriwal and his fellow activists. These protests attracted lower participation than the ones organized in 2011. By mid 2012, Kejriwal replaced Anna Hazare as the face of the remaining protestors.[45]

Gareth Smith[46] considered political parties and/ or politicians to be brands because of their resemblance to commercial organizations in their exchange of ideas and promises of support. However, the complexity of products offered by political parties (from commitments on development, economy, overseas aid, health, education, defence, employment and so on) limits the application of a branding concept in politics. Another concern is that policies offered/promised by political parties during election campaigning might be watered down once these parties get elected.

The main roles of branding in political marketing are pursuing consumers (voters), meaning that they are consumer oriented; understanding the way in which a brand (political leader) is affecting consumers; directing the efforts of the organization in promoting the brand as a power brand; and attracting consumers. Consumers are becoming increasingly aware of where to best invest their money (in this case cast their vote) for the long-term, and brand knowledge simplifies their choice of a leader in the complex system of politics.

Brand knowledge is a complex network of information. Current events are constantly being associated with previous events and, in this manner, a brand image is created in the consumer's mind. For example, seeing Modi on TV can trigger associations with the BJP, 'Vibrant Gujarat' and so on. That is how the star campaigner or brand personality is seen as an aligned network, relating to the leader's characteristics and political party, retrieved from the memory of a voter when stimulated by a current event.

Brand personality is an important component of a brand's image. Personality is defined as 'the set of meanings constructed by an observer to describe the "inner" characteristics of another person',[47] and brand personality is 'the set of human characteristics associated with a brand'.[48] The voter's behaviour towards the political knowledge he or she has gained determines the perception of a brand's personality.

In politics, brand personality is described by a model in which partisanship is considered the moderator. Partisanship is associated with four major factors: events, politician/party actions, advertising and brand user/advertisers. These factors determine the impact of brand-personality knowledge on people's voting intentions. Brand personality also helps voters decide when they want to differentiate among potential leaders and make wise choices based on trust or perceived personality of the leader and his or her party.

The purpose of campaigning is to highlight a party's ideology and to emphasize the personality traits of party leaders, not to show the real personality of a campaigner. The party offers leaders an umbrella of traits, such as reliance, togetherness and recognition. A party's brand heritage (popular elements of a brand's history, influence and perception) and current policies affect the perceived brand personality. Parties and their leaders both have an associated effect on a voter's memory, and the voter considers both to be an overall brand.

A political party's identity is judged by party members' personalities, its supporters and the actions of the party's leaders over a defined period of time. As described in limited brand personality scale, honesty, leadership, image, uniqueness, spiritedness and toughness are all important to being a star campaigner in the political marketplace. Honesty seems to be more important when it comes to delivering promises on a wider scale. In the case of politics, honesty is frequently questioned by the media and the Opposition parties. Dimensions like image and leadership are defined by traits like confidence and intelligence, which are closely related to an individual rather than the whole party. Uniqueness is considered to be a party asset.[49]

The three main challenges that the BJP had to overcome in projecting Modi as a star campaigner and a prime-ministerial candidate were: transitioning from regional to national leader, connecting with the youth, and the impact of the Gujarat riots on his image. Senior BJP leaders and advertising legends were responsible for handling the BJP's marketing and Modi's branding and promotion. Two benchmark events in the crafting of Modi's national image were the shifting of Tata Motors' Nano minicar factory from West Bengal to Gujarat in 2008 as well as how quickly the government provided the company with land and workers and the farmers with incentives.

The gradual downfall of Congress as a national brand and the nation's fundamental requirement for change both helped Modi rise as a BJP brand personality. Even though he was well known outside Gujarat, as a part of his political campaign, Modi still ventured into different states to participate in around 470 political rallies and more than 5000 events across the country. Modi continued to become a national icon and attract the youth vote when he spoke on development, the importance of youth in economic growth and employment at Delhi's Shri Ram College of Commerce on 6 February 2013. While the catchword 'NaMo' attracted many Hindu voters, the clear development agenda of Modi earned him the praise of top industrialists and urban voters. The above examples indicate that through various approaches and strategies, Modi branded himself as a progressive (neoteric) leader with the ability to deliver significant results.

The biggest advantage of these personalized campaigns is that they cut through the Indian system's bias factors and impress the heterogeneous population by breaking the social barriers. This campaign strategy differed from those of earlier leaders, which focused more on caste, creed and religion. Instead of defending allegations based on his tainted past, Modi kept quiet on the issue, concentrating on his recent history and strong image.[50]

Negative Image in Action

Clinton–Lewinsky Controversy

Bill Clinton was the second President in US history to be impeached by the House of Representatives. The famous controversy regarding his sexual affair with a twenty-two-year-old White House intern rocked the world from 1997 to 1998. After the Clinton–Lewinsky controversy, a conservative senator described Clinton as a 'nasty, bad, naughty boy'[51]. The life of a politician is always under scrutiny. If these allegations were true, they would question Clinton's judgement, his self-control, his character and even his stability. Bill Clinton survived so many seemingly fatal reversals that few in Washington predicted that this would capsize his political career. Even so, many of his most ardent defenders understood that these charges presented Clinton with his career's most formidable challenge. Public Broadcasting Service (PBS) recently released the first half of a documentary on Clinton, covering everything from his broken childhood in Arkansas to his rise as one of the most successful politicians in modern American history. Clinton is one of the most complex and conflicted political characters ever to walk across the public stage,[52] and the Lewinsky scandal is not the only one of its kind to have made headlines. As depicted in the documentary, Clinton was involved in other such incidents when he was the Governor of Arkansas. Because of these allegations, his campaign manager once even advised him not to run for President.

One of Clinton's other advisers said in the documentary, 'I said to him that the problem that presidents have is not the sin, it's the cover-up. You should explore just telling the American people the truth.'[53] Clinton rejected his advice, but a poll conducted by the adviser confirms its validity. The results indicated that 'voters would have been willing to forgive the affair, but not the fact that they had been lied to'. According to Pulitzer Prize winner David Maraniss, 'With Bill Clinton it is tempting but often misleading to try to separate good from bad . . . he is by far the smartest politician I have encountered, he can recall a phone number he has not dialled in 30 years. He has a brilliant memory for everything except for his own history and how to deal with it.'[54]

On 17 August 1998, Clinton became the first sitting President to testify before a grand jury investigating his conduct. Eventually, he admitted his inappropriate relationship with Monica Lewinsky on national television. Based on evidence submitted by an independent counsel, the jury decided to impeach Clinton on two charges—obstruction of justice and abuse of power.[55]

Coca-Cola

Coca-Cola is the world's largest beverage company and the biggest brand. The company is committed to using its resources to improve the conditions for their international business partners. In 2009, Coca-Cola launched its 'Live Positively' campaign as part of its worldwide commitment to give back to the communities in which it operates. The project aimed to promote sustainability in the world, focusing on global issues like climate change, education, balanced living and women's empowerment. The project was launched in Brazil, India, South Africa and the Philippines.

'The Best Coke That I *Ever* Had Was' campaign asked consumers to share their experiences online and, as part of the 'Open Happiness' campaign, the 'Moments of Happiness' portal allowed people to share photographs that spread 'happiness.'[56] People enjoy Coca-Cola beverages, which are basically a combination of sugar or artificial sweeteners and carbonated water. Such products have been scrutinized by individuals and in some cases by environmentalists on the grounds of harmful effects on health. These messages were largely circulated through media and medical advisers in public domain. In any case, the company has responded positively to most negative communications on their brand.

Being Raw or Being Real

While most companies routinely apologize if problems are detected in their products, Modi did not do so. 'He did give an account of reflections on the event [the riots]. He seemed to say that he was pained about the event but didn't say sorry,' says Y.L.R Moorthi[57]. Similarly, Prahlad Kakkar, a man who has been involved in many political campaigns, including one for the late prime minister Indira Gandhi, observed, 'It does not matter if he [Modi] is wrong. He will never publicly admit that—but he will, at the same time, take corrective measures to navigate out of it, without ever saying so.'[58]

Not long ago, Modi was described as authoritarian, megalomaniac and communal. However, the creators of Modi's brand handled this situation differently, manipulating it to work out in Modi's favour. They focused on building an image of Modi as self-made, strong, efficient, inspiring and incorruptible. Ramadhar Singh, a social scientist and a distinguished professor at IIM Bangalore, remarked, 'He [Modi] created an impression of being a sincere, credible and committed leader. He convinced people that he could improve their lot.'[59] Veteran adman Prahlad Kakkar adds, 'No media can help create that kind of consistency.' At this same time, the Congress-led United Progressive Alliance (UPA) began to look more and more indecisive and corrupt. 'Today, India attributes weakness and failure to Congress while Modi stands for good governance,' says adman and lobbyist Suhel Seth.[60]

Practically, all the stories about Modi's life, which were in the public domain, have consistently fed into this new image. Although there are still questions about Modi's ability to perform at the national level and about the model of his governance in Gujarat, his personal branding and marketing strategy seem to have worked; voters across the country appear to believe his claims. 'Even if you cut out 40 per cent of what is untrue about Modi's promise of growth . . . the rest is very real,' says Guwahati's Chiranjib Hazarika.[61]

AAP contested 69 seats of Delhi legislative assembly election in 2013, won 28. Bhartiya Janta Party contested 66 seats, won 31, INC contested 70 seats and won only 8. As no party won the clear majority of 70 seats in the assembly, Delhi was put under president's rule until next election. The AAP conducted a survey in Delhi to gauge the public mood before taking the support of Congress, a party they historically disagreed with. The survey showed that the public was in favour of forming the government when the opportunity existed while excluding Congress in actual government functioning. Finally, Kejriwal accepted Congress's offer and agreed to form a government. He was sworn in as the 7th chief minister of Delhi on 28 December 2013.[62]

Kejriwal's forty-nine days as the chief minister of Delhi were heavily scrutinized by the media, putting unmanageable pressure on him to perform well. His lack of governmental experience also influenced this period.

One of his first decisions after becoming the chief minister was to slash electricity consumption charges by 50 per cent for up to 400 units consumed. The Opposition deemed this as populist and devoid of sound economic sense because the subsidy was to come from taxpayers' money. He also announced that all households in Delhi would receive twenty kilolitres of free water and vowed to curb the water-tanker mafias that were prevalent amongst certain localities of Delhi without water pipelines. The Opposition again termed this decision impractical and impossible to implement. The AAP government also opposed the foreign direct investment (FDI) in multi-brand retail that the UPA government was pushing for. Kejriwal also set up an anti-corruption helpline in an effort to take prompt action in corruption cases.

The heaviest criticism levelled during Kejriwal's term as CM followed his protest on 20 January 2014 at Rail Bhavan against the Union home ministry. This protest came after Delhi Law Minister Somnath Bharti conducted a midnight raid in the localities, which were inhabited by a large number of African immigrants.[63] Residents had complained to the minister that these immigrants were involved in drug trafficking and other illegal activities. The minister alleged that he found evidence of such activities during a visit and that he did not observe any prevention attempts by the local police. This incident was recorded on video, and the recording of the arguments between Somnath Bharti and the police went viral the next day. After this incident, Kejriwal demanded that the police come under direct control of the Delhi government and that the officers who refused to do as Bharti requested be suspended. He said that the protest would not hamper his work, as he had brought along files and would carry on working from the venue of the protest.

Kejriwal claimed to be the first chief minister to protest on the streets, demanding fair inquiry. After two days, he ended his protest when Lieutenant Governor Najeeb Jung intervened by sending the two police officers involved on leave and confirming the setting up of a judicial inquiry. This whole affair left an awful taste in general public's mouth, who thought the CM's intentions were good, but did not approve of his methods.

Some of Arvind Kejriwal's prepoll statements—like his promise to deny extra police security and government accommodation—came back to haunt him whenever he acted even slightly incongruously. He was painted as 'Mr U-turn' for continuously going back on his own words and an 'anarchist' because of his penchant for protests and dharnas.

Kejriwal decided to contest Narendra Modi in the general elections from Varanasi. After a high-voltage campaign, he lost the election by a landslide. His short stint in Delhi was seen as a way to propel his interests in national politics.[64]

AAP as a unit also fared badly during the Lok Sabha elections of 2014. The party fielded 434 candidates throughout the country in an attempt to ride on the anti-incumbency factor against the UPA government and spread its presence in as many parts of the country as possible. They also thought that by contesting for so many seats nationwide, they would at least be given national party status by the Election Commission of India.

However, the outcome was disastrous. As many had predicted, the newly-formed party was not prepared to face such an uphill task, and their resources were stretched way beyond their limits. Only four out of 434 AAP candidates won the election, all of them from the same state, Punjab. The party obtained only 2 per cent of all the votes that were cast, and 414 of its candidates forfeited their deposit by failing to secure one-sixth of the votes in their constituencies. Although they performed relatively well in Delhi by securing 32.9 per cent of the votes, they still failed to win any seats. This decision proved to be suicidal for AAP and the party took a big blow on its brand image.

Immediately after the elections, many people, who had joined the party during its rise to prominence, left. Shazia Ilmi, one of the party's founders, resigned, alleging that the party was run by a select few and had no internal democracy. Arvind Kejriwal was again criticized for being an autocrat and for not respecting the women. The ideologue and another founder member of AAP, Yogendra Yadav, also criticized the leadership style of Arvind Kejriwal in an open letter, writing that party members deviated from their objectives, falling prey to the personality cult of Kejriwal.

Image Makeover

Just like every organization is exposed to accidental crisis, so are the images of personalities. Understanding how crisis communication can be used to protect reputational assets during a crisis is crucial to understanding crisis management.[65] Situational crisis communication theory (SCCT) projects how people will react to strategies adopted for crisis management.

Image is vital to organizations as well as for individuals. In the field of public relations, image is considered to be a central concept. Reputation is widely regarded as a valuable and an intangible asset. For an organization, it can attract customers (followers in the case of an individual), investment interest and the best of talent. It can improve financial performance, increase returns on assets and create a competitive advantage. While understanding the concept of image restoration discourse, it is important to know the image repair efforts of individuals and companies. The vital fact about image repair in case of organizations is that it can bring larger resources than individuals can. Image restoration discourse largely focuses on options for messages.

The theory offers five broad categories of image repair strategy:

S. No.	Strategy	Characteristics
1.	Denial • Simple denial • Shift the blame	 • Did not perform the act • Act performed by another
2.	Evasion of responsibility • Provocation • Defensibility • Accident • Good intentions	 • Responded to act of another • Lack of information or ability • Act was a mishap • Meant well in act
3.	Reducing offensiveness of event • Bolstering • Minimization • Differentiation • Transcendence • Attack accuser • Compensation	 • Stress good traits • Act not serious • Act less offensive • More important considerations • Reduce credibility of accuser • Reimburse victim
4.	Corrective action	• Plan to solve or prevent problem
5.	Mortification	• Apologies for act

Source: Benoit, William L., 'Image Repair Discourse and Crisis Communication', *Public Relations Review* 23: 2, 1997, pp. 177–86.

In his 1997 article, Benoit argues, 'In the process of restoring image after the crisis, like organizations, individuals should also be able to anticipate the potential crisis and hence prepare contingency plans. This plan must be reviewed periodically, updated and implemented attentively.'[66]

One should be able to understand both the nature of the crisis and the relevant audience(s). If an individual or firm knows the nature of the crisis, then an appropriate response can be applied to handle the same. In other words, the response must be tailored to the offence. While handling the crisis, it is key that the 'message' be communicated. There will be more than one stakeholder, such as customers, investors, community, government, etc. The message that is conveyed may please one section of the audience but not the other. This can be taken care of by communicating different messages to different groups.[67]

David Aaker, American marketing guru and author of several books on branding, wrote a blog post explaining that every person has a brand. Their brand affects how they are perceived and whether they are liked and respected. According to him, this brand can either be actively managed with discipline and consistency or be allowed to drift. Modi and his marketing team demonstrated both discipline and consistency when he was appointed the BJP's prime-ministerial candidate on 13 September 2013. In fact, the team had started working on the same much before.[68]

Modi's transformation in 2012-13[69], from being a right-wing politician to a decisive leader with a clear development agenda, demonstrates the type of extraordinary effort that is well suited to advancing India. Senior BJP leaders Piyush Goyal and Ajay Singh handled the overall media strategy, and a task force was constructed to handle Modi's campaign in Varanasi, the constituency from which Modi contested. Advertising legends such as Ogilvy & Mather's Piyush Pandey, McCann Worldgroup's Prasoon Joshi and Sam Balsara of Madison World lent their skills at various levels, and the advertising agency Soho Square, part of the WPP Group, handled Modi's television, radio and print campaigns with catchy slogans such as 'Abki Baar, Modi Sarkar'[It will be Modi's government this time].

According to Y.L.R. Moorthi, professor of marketing at the Indian Institute of Management, Bengaluru, there is a difference between a regional brand going national and a politician going national. Before he decided to move beyond the state of Gujarat, Modi was known nationally in the same way that Nitish Kumar and J. Jayalalithaa, chief ministers of Bihar and Tamil Nadu, respectively, were known. Yet these regional leaders did not venture out of their home states in the recent elections, whereas Modi did at a massive scale, attending more than 5000 events and 470 political rallies across the length and breadth of the country.[70]

Modi, an excellent orator, has delivered scores of wildly influential speeches. He highlighted the slowing economic growth of the country, high inflation and a lack of new jobs—issues that immediately resonate with young and urban voters—and blamed the Congress-led UPA government. After the elections were announced, his marketing team bombarded voters with print, television and radio advertisements on the same themes. Advertisements even reached voters through text messages featuring Modi's recorded voice. To magnify the impact of the advertising and the branding campaign, the team also used social media platforms such as Facebook, YouTube and Twitter. In the run-up to the election, Modi had about forty lakh Twitter followers.

The biggest challenge that Modi's brand faced was diverting the public's attention away from the 2002 communal riots in

Gujarat that claimed the lives of more than 1000 people, most of whom were Muslims. Initially, Modi's supporters in the BJP attempted to engage in public debate, highlighting the clean chit given by courts in an effort to wash off the stigma. Later, they changed their approach and toned down the Hindutva rhetoric, instead focusing on Modi's recent achievements and his development record in Gujarat.

Another example is that of Zulfikar Ali Bhutto, who became the foreign minister of Pakistan in 1963. After falling out with the then President Ayub Khan, Z.A. Bhutto formed the separate Pakistan People's Party and stated its belief as 'Islam is our Faith, Democracy is our Policy, Socialism is our Economy, All Power to the People.'[71]

As described by Anwar Syed, Z.A. Bhutto achieved victory in 1970 to become the prime minister of Pakistan with the help of his self-characterization in political campaigns.[72] In his political campaigns, he would characterize himself as:

1. Competent: During his campaigns, he used to project himself as a person with high educational credentials and as a powerful politician capable of ruling the country.

2. Brave: He represented himself as a courageous and fearless person who had the potential to reduce the social and economic problems of his country and its citizens.

3. Democrat: He always represented himself as a democrat, treating all Pakistanis as his family members. He referred to himself as a true nationalist of Pakistan.

4. Principled and upright: In his campaigns, he used to represent himself as a 'man of principles', touting his honesty, virtuousness and trustworthiness.

5. Man for the people: In his every speech, he presented himself as a 'man for the people'. He stated that 'he was a

servant of the people, their brother, friend and spokesman', making him worthy of being their leader.

6. India resistant: In his election campaigns, he used to refer to India as an 'enemy to Islam and Muslims'. He portrayed himself as a fearless leader and promised Pakistani citizens to contest India on Kashmir-related issues. All this gave a boost to his popularity as a true Muslim leader to the country.

7. Socialist servant of Islam: He considered himself to be a true socialist, and according to him only socialism could eradicate the hardships of Pakistan. He also portrayed himself as a true devotee of Islam.

Marketing gurus cite the examples of Cadbury, PepsiCo and Coca-Cola, which all battled problems relating to brand taint. Cadbury fought its way out of a controversy related to worms in its chocolates, while the two beverage giants faced allegations that their colas contained pesticides. 'The best way for a tainted brand to overcome a challenge is to not talk too much, but to acknowledge it happened, and then move on,' says Samu, a professor at Indian School of Business. 'The more one talks about it, the more the memory for that event gets activated among the target market, and they remember it more. The BJP and Modi did not talk about it. Or if they did, they kept it to a minimum,' he adds.[73]

Image Repair in Action

Suggestions for effective image repair:

1. Persuasion: Avoid making false claims and provide adequate support for all claims. Campaigns, if any, should

   be developed with a theme and not around arguments. For
   example, Coke's response to Pepsi's accusations.

2. Immediate acceptance of fault: It is advisable to accept
   one's fault. It must be decided by the organization whether
   they would rather save the image or avoid litigation.
   For example, Pepsi should have apologized to Coke for
   making false accusations, or Union Carbide should have
   taken some responsibility for the gas leak in Bhopal. Yet,
   on occasions the accused is innocent. Tylenol successfully
   denied their responsibility for the deaths of the consumers.

3. Shifting the blame successfully: In case of Tylenol, the
   company shifted the blame for the poisoning to an
   unknown and insane person.

4. Strategy of defeasibility: Benoit argues that if factors
   beyond one's control can be shown to have caused the
   offensive act, this may help restore a tarnished image.[74]

5. Announcing plans to avoid similar problems: Companies
   who have admitted to a fault or mistake must then report
   plans to correct and/or prevent the recurrence of the
   problem. For example, Tylenol first denied responsibility
   for the deaths that occurred from the poisoned capsules,
   but later they also introduced new tamper-resistant
   packaging.

Toyota Motor Corporation faced a major challenge selling their
cars in the US as they did not effectively manage public relations
in the country. The company's mismanagement resulted in
lawsuits, testimony before the Congress, diminished brand
image, diminished reputation and financial loss. In addition,
the company incurred heavy loss in terms of shareholder
value. Some of the reports suggest that the company knew
about this problem well in advance but did not have a CEO

in the US. The crisis situation required constructive action. Toyota has a centralized decision-making and organizational structure. The company's US unit had not been empowered to make the final decision. We can infer from this situation that Japanese engineers had been isolated from the concerns of US customers.

Toyota's global expansion achieved speed and scale at the cost of global coordination. In the initial years of their expansion strategy, they achieved global standardization and efficiency but lacked local responsiveness. Norman Austine[75] offers a set of guidelines for crisis management:

1. Avoiding the crisis
2. Preparing to manage the crisis
3. Recognizing the crisis
4. Containing the crisis
5. Resolving the crisis
6. Profiting from the crisis

The company's president, Akio Toyoda, took personal ownership of the problem and initiated a company rescue. Toyoda did apply some the above mentioned measures, but he failed largely at most of them. The media attention brought on by this crisis denigrated the company's image. Toyota is synonymous with quality; so all quality-related issues became part of the problem.

Another example is that of Johnson & Johnson's Tylenol, which was promoted as an over-the-counter drug in 1980 and it soon became the flagship product of the company with the help of aggressive promotion. In the autumn of 1982, McNeil Consumer Products, a subsidiary of Johnson & Johnson (J&J), was confronted with a crisis when seven people in Chicago's

West Side died mysteriously. Authorities determined that all of the people who died had ingested an Extra-Strength Tylenol capsule laced with cyanide. The news of this incident travelled quickly, causing massive, nationwide panic.

Authorities suspected some kind of tampering at the J&J plant or in the distribution chains, particularly those located near the Chicago area. It was a huge blow to J&J's image and their flagship brand Tylenol. J&J immediately decided to launch a public-relations programme to save the integrity of both their product and corporation across the nation. It was a classic case of face-saving-communication strategy. J&J immediately announced through the media that everyone should stop consuming any kind of Tylenol drug. They recalled all existing Tylenol capsules from the market and halted production of the drug till the tampering was detected.

The entire strategy was planned in two stages.

Stage 1:

1. Advising consumers across the nation to stop the consumption of any type of Tylenol product.
2. Banning the advertisement for Tylenol.
3. Immediately announcing product recall from the market (value approx. $100 million).
4. Establishing contacts with the Federal Bureau of Investigation (FBI), Chicago police and the Food and Drug Administration (FDA) to tackle the problem.

The first stage of this communication policy was to halt further damage to brand image. By taking such measures, J&J succeeded in their strategy. Media praised J&J for their commitment towards society. Their efforts were also praised by authors like Jerry Knight in the *Washington Post*.

These were quite unusual steps for a large company like J&J. In many similar cases, companies had put themselves first; they ended up doing more damage to their reputation than they would have if immediate responsibility for the crisis had been taken.[76]

Stage 2:

1. Reintroduction of Tylenol capsules with improved packaging.
2. Immediate compliance with new FDA policy.
3. Discount coupons for consumers.
4. Presentations by J&J sales people to the medical community (target audience).

This strategy was well received both by the consumers and the media. The strategy was supported by new advertising campaigns across the states to promote the initiative taken by J&J. Additionally, J&J received free publicity from the many authors who wrote extensively about its strategies. According to market reports published in newspapers, in a very short time span after the crisis, Tylenol regained 24 per cent of the market share, compared to its pre-crisis 37 per cent share.

Takeaway

Tylenol clearly handled this situation effectively. J&J knew that restoring customer faith was a big challenge and immediate measures needed to be taken to quickly stop any further damage. J&J also understood that the media would be involved in such a case, taking a decisive role. They used the media to spread messages across the country with only specific information.

Crisis brings along the problem of loss of consumer trust and calls into question a company's integrity. To counter this in the Tylenol case, J&J voluntarily brought in all major governmental and legal agencies to assist them in sorting out the case. J&J directly sent a message to the consumers that the company was not involved in any wrongdoing and was, furthermore, willing to help people. As mentioned earlier, the media extensively wrote about and praised J&J's communication strategy. This provided free publicity to the company's efforts.

In the course of image makeover after any crisis, establishing one-on-one dialogue with the stakeholders is vital. For a big corporation like J&J this was a Herculean task, which they effectively tackled by ensuring that their sales people talked to the medical fraternity and reinstated faith in the brand. Drawing an analogue to this situation, Modi's 'Chai pe Charcha' represents a similar strategy.

* * *

The above discussion of negative publicity and contortions of speech suggests that when communicating with the public, one's language is as important as one's message. Research in management suggests that different uses of language in political speeches affect listeners in different ways. The manner in which a politician frames his or her speech can affect the interpretation process of the listeners. This concept arose from research in social psychology, which indicates that the language people use to describe other people's behaviour can affect the inferences drawn by the receivers.

Research suggests that using concrete communication to handle negative messages about politicians can lead to more favourable responses from prospective voters.[77] Similarly, when politicians use abstract communication to handle negative messages disseminated about them, it tends to elicit unfavourable responses from prospective voters.

Abstract Communication

'Shun all the sins committed so far, give up that way, follow the way of goodwill and brotherhood, and let`s resolve to take the country forward. I believe we can do that.'—Narendra Modi[78]

'There is a little bit of fear. Narendra Modi is a powerful person. I am speaking well.'—Rahul Gandhi[79]

'How is that the statue of Gandhi stands outside the British parliament? To that question my answer is: the British are wise enough to recognize his greatness and Indians are generous enough to share him.'—Narendra Modi[80]

'For this purpose we opened 140 million bank accounts, increased FDI in insurance upto 49% and have set up Mudra Bank to fund the microbusinesses'—Narendra Modi[81]

'There were attempts to spark riots, one church was torched, some were attacked. Delhi's residents are peace loving. In the past 35 years, we haven't seen such incidents.'—Arvind Kejriwal[82]

Concrete Communication

Source: Language abstraction in political communication based on Semin and Fiedler's linguistic category model, 1988.[83]

According to the above diagram, when the level of abstraction increases in public communications, the message not only becomes less concrete but also less effective. We conducted a content analysis of over 1100 speeches made by Narendra Modi, Rahul Gandhi, Mamata Banerjee and Mulayam Singh Yadav. We found that Modi's speeches contained 82 per cent concrete messages, whereas the speeches of Rahul Gandhi, Mamata Banerjee and Mulayam Singh Yadav were composed of 24 per cent, 28 per cent and 20 per cent concrete content respectively.

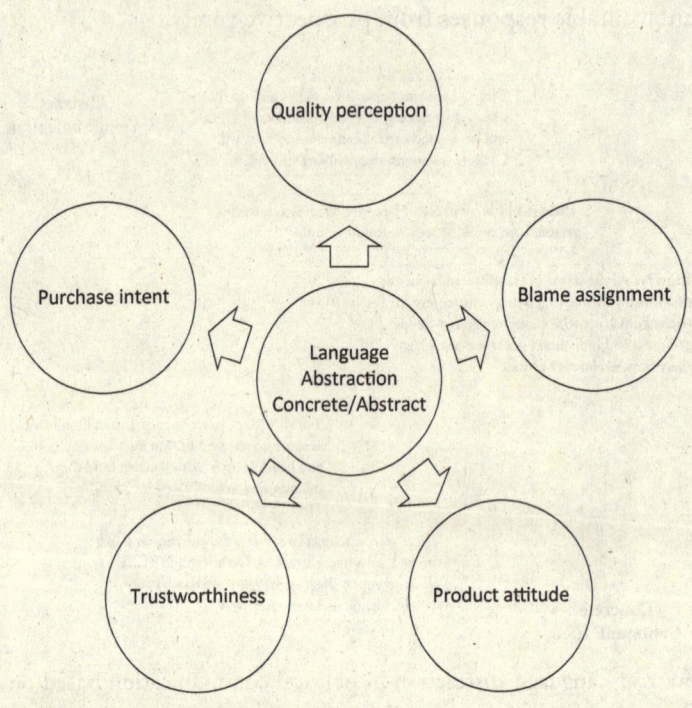

Another model dealing with the implications of language abstraction on voters is as follows. Language abstraction affects the quality of perception, blame assignment, attitude towards a product (in this case a candidate or party), trustworthiness and purchase intent (in this case intention to vote). The more concrete a candidate's language is, the higher the public opinion of that candidate is, the less blame they are assigned, the more trustworthy they seem and the more people intend to vote for them. Language used in political communications makes a huge difference and should be given ample importance. In terms of image management, the lessons that can be drawn from the Toyota example are: first, the importance of achieving coordination and control and, second, the importance of culture, which acts as a glue that sticks coordination and control.

MANAGING WORKFORCE

The Art of Apology

When to Apologize

There are situations when things go wrong, they do not happen as expected or many people get hurt unintentionally. While it is hard to accept our mistakes and failure, an apology is expected in such situations.[1] Being a political leader, such acceptance is even more difficult; it can harm the position and image of their party in the public domain. In such situations, a good leader will act wisely by defending himself or herself in a strong and thoughtful way. An apology at the right time allows him or her to negotiate with and positively influence people.[2]

A perfect example of this is Arvind Kejriwal, who apologized after quitting the position of Delhi's chief minister after forty-nine days. He agreed that his actions were not supported by the people of Delhi and that he could not deliver what he had promised at the time of the elections. He said that he would hold a fresh round of elections to give Delhi residents a fair chance to decide their ruling political party. His apology had both immediate and long-term effects. The immediate effect was that the people of Delhi did not vote for AAP in the 2014 Lok Sabha elections. However, the new government's workings allowed Delhi residents to realize the AAP's contribution during those forty-nine days and, as a result, the AAP won the 2015 state assembly elections by an enormous margin. This can be seen as the long-term effect of Kejriwal's apology.[3]

Another example is that of Bihar's chief minister Nitish Kumar. He sincerely apologized to the people of Bihar and to his party workers for his resignation as the chief minister of Bihar and the subsequent crowning of Jitan Ram Manjhi as the new chief minister. He also stated that the incapable BJP government would not be able to rule Bihar in the upcoming elections. The apology had a positive impact on the people of Bihar, and the BJP started to lose the trust they had built there.[4]

When Not to Apologize

The above examples indicate that making a timely public apology has helped many political leaders regain their lost reputation, winning them public sympathy. On the other hand, there are instances when politicians have refused to apologize for their deeds. Taking such a stance can sometimes backfire. In such situations, an aggressive attitude might create a problem that did not exist in the first place. But, there are a few leaders who have maintained this attitude very well, winning millions of hearts.

For example, Prime Minister Narendra Modi was charged for his involvement in the 2002 Gujarat riots but he maintained a non-apologizing stance. He said that if the people in Gujarat felt he was guilty, he should be hanged to death; not left with a punishment as small as a public apology.[5]

How to Apologize?

In a crisis situation, the decision whether a politician should apologize or not becomes more crucial. Once this decision to apologize is made, there are various ways in which the apology can be executed. In such a scenario, pulling off the apology well is crucial. If an apology has not been delivered sincerely and genuinely, it can negatively impact the target audience. Instead of building a better image of the politician in their minds, the apology might seem fake and people might feel cheated.

There are a few things that a politician or a leader must keep in mind when making an apology. One should ensure that the apology reaches the right people at the right time and the right place. As advised in the field of medicine as well, one should be clear about the facts of the case and be willing to explain the entire situation again; addressing what went wrong and what steps will be taken to ensure that a similar situation will not arise in the future.[6]

To Whom to Apologize?

The apology should be made to all the stakeholders. In case of a politician, the stakeholders are the voters, the various leaders of the political party and the ministers of the assembly. To some extent, members of the Opposition and the allied parties also act as the stakeholders. The politician must ensure that the apology is directed to the most affected stakeholder and that the stakeholder is convinced by his or her apology.

Every apology has a purpose. An apology without a purpose and directed to the wrong audience is a disaster. Such an apology will spoil not only the image of the politician, but also that of the other people associated with him or her. It will degrade the name of the political party. Thus it is crucial to a politician's survival in this complicated and unpredictable world of politics that they learn the art of apology.

Image Building

Modi has always emphasized the rapid progress of Gujarat and secularism. He wanted people to acknowledge and weigh the benefits of the development model implemented by him in his state. His development model is based on 'sadbhavana'. It conveys that the development and growth of any sector or section of society can be achieved by peace, unity and brotherhood. To replace the age-old practice of divide and rule, he gave the mantra 'Collective Effort, Inclusive Growth' for societal development. Modi emphasized the four pillars (security, equality, prosperity and equity) on which Gujarat had been built over the last ten years.[7]

To be a strong candidate for the prime-ministerial elections, it was imperative that Modi's team projected an image of him as a fair, strong and influential politician. There was a conscious effort to segregate religion from secularism. In other words, Modi's message indicated that while he respected all religions, he was proud of his own religion. This message was communicated in various rallies and public appearances and can be observed in the speeches that he delivered across the country.

'I will never go by this terminology of yours. Even if you drag me, I will not. I will meet my countrymen. I understand only one language that they are my countrymen, they are my brothers. You may see with whatever colour you want, Modi will not go into that colour,' conveyed Modi in one of his speeches. He also stated that it was his responsibility to reach all parts of the society, including Muslims. In his election manifesto, he promised to restore Muslim heritage sites and committed to promoting Muslim education. About the 2002 Gujarat riots, Modi said he passed the test and was ready for another but would never surrender before lies and political motives.[8]

In the Indian political space, there have always been controversies regarding the secular credentials of politicians and their parties. The BJP and specifically Modi have been often perceived in a negative light in such controversies.

During his general election campaign in May 2014, Modi was questioned by many secular intellectuals about performing 'Ganga Aarti',[9] a specific Hindu religious rite. This was connected to his Sadbhavana Mission and refusal to wear a 'skull cap'—a distinctively Muslim religious symbol.[10] Modi, in his public discourse, never shied away from presenting himself as a proud Hindu man and spoke often of the difference between being religious and being secular.

In fact, during an interview with the *Hindustan Times* he coined the term 'Hindu nationalist', which encapsulated his views on religion, secularism and nationalism.'I'm a nationalist. I'm patriotic. Nothing is wrong. I'm a born Hindu. So yes, you can say I'm a Hindu nationalist.' He further added, 'As far as progressive, development-oriented, workaholic . . . there's no contradiction between the two. It is one and the same image.'[11]

Promoting Women's Safety and Security

Delhi was simmering with fury after the death of a young woman who was gang-raped on a bus in New Delhi. On this note, the prime minister's biggest agenda was to ensure women's safety and to project an image of himself as one who could guarantee this in India.

Modi spoke frequently on women's safety and his policies around women's empowerment to win the favour of Indian women. Modi insisted that women's development was the key to societal development. He initiated many women's empowerment programmes under his governance such as 'Beti Bachao Campaign' to increase the sex ratio in the state, 'Gaurav Nari Niti' to increase women's participation in all fields of work, 'Balika Samruddhi Yojana' to promote girl child and 'Kishori Shakti Yojna' to provide nutrition along with education.[12] Society saw these initiatives as steps in the right direction in terms of women's empowerment and safety.

Mud-slinging is a common practice in Indian politics.[13] Research shows that the public is not impressed with such antics and that they prefer a neutral leader who is focused on development. Modi wanted to ensure that he was portrayed as a leader who was extremely down to earth and did not believe in belittling his opposition. At the same time, he maintained his image as a forward-thinking politician who did not believe in scraping the past and magnifying issues.

Modi obliged his senior leaders and allies by speaking about them during or after his political speeches. He also showed the nation that he remembered the contributions of the senior leaders, even when he was victorious. This genuine effort was made by Modi to project himself as a grass-roots leader.[14]

He attempted to appear as a statesman to the public rather than a party politician. He maintained an image of optimism. Rather than blaming any of the previous governments' workings, he communicated that every government had served the nation in its own way. He also did not miss any opportunity to praise the previous governments' work and he believed in continuing it. Modi assured the public that he would not leave any stone unturned in his efforts to fulfil his responsibility to the nation.

The increasingly mature Indian citizens accepted these traits. Modi was projected as a mature and a dynamic leader with a strong sense of morality.

To Be Projected as a Clean Leader

The Indian public was mainly concerned with the processes of the current bureaucratic governance. Indian politics is famous for its corrupt practices and slow work development at the government offices. Narendra Modi ensured that his quick decision-making would result in a clean bureaucratic system. This painted him as a man of action.

Narendra Modi made several remarks on good governance and development, often stating that there are no alternatives to good governance. His government implemented an appraisal system for ministers, which included certain requirements—ministers would have to be rated in a 'common style' evaluation every year. Such actions bolstered his image as that of a decisive leader with the ability to clean up the Indian polity and executive bodies.[15]

To Be Projected as a Leader with a Positive Attitude

Indian politics is associated with corruption, bureaucracy and red-tapism. All these traits have a negative connotation. Narendra Modi ensured that he was looked at as a man with an extremely positive attitude. He ensured that he uplifted the mood of the entire Indian society by giving them the sense that there were great things ahead. He made an effort to separate his image from that of a conventional Indian politician, painting his thinking process as progressive when compared to other politicians.

Modi displayed half a glass of water and asked the audience what they saw. He told them that optimists see this as a glass half filled with water, while pessimists see it as half empty. He attempted to ensure that people acknowledged that he was different, announcing that he was a man of unlimited possibilities and claiming, '*Yeh glass khali nahi hai, yeh glass aadha paani se aur aadha hawa se bhara hai* [This glass is not empty. It is half filled with water and half with air].' Statements such as these greatly affected the audience, and he successfully projected himself as a man who could think differently. Modi ensured that he was seen to have a positive attitude towards the smaller things in life.[16]

He made efforts to project himself as a leader rather than just a representative of a political party. He worked on developing his image as a leader and not that of a politician wooing voters or attacking the Opposition with sarcastic comments.

To Be Projected as People's Leader

It is well known that great leaders are those who can touch, move and inspire people. To do so one must reach out to them. Modi projected himself as a leader, who is always available for the public, by participating in several rallies during his campaign as well as by meeting people.

From September 2013 to April 2014, Modi appeared in a total of 5827 public-interfacing events and travelled across twenty-five states to connect with the public. Modi attended 437 big rallies and gave additional time to people with particular queries. Most of his rallies were overflowed with thousands of supporters. He wanted to be known as a people-friendly and approachable minister of state. Modi also conveyed to the public that the fruit of the victory would not take him away from his roots, and that he, as a human being, would always remain the same as he was before becoming the prime minister of the country. Even on 16 May, when the results of the 2014 general elections were announced, he said that 'he was always a call away', thus giving assurance that he would always remain close to the people. He committed himself to reduce the gap between him and the people of the nation.[17]

Modi could be described as a 'charismatic leader'. Many of history's most effective leaders such as Mahatma Gandhi, Martin Luther King Jr and Winston Churchill have also been labelled as charismatic leaders. According to management literature, charismatic leaders are essentially very skilled communicators—individuals who are not only verbally eloquent, but are also able to communicate with followers at a deep and emotional level. They can articulate a compelling or captivating vision and can arouse strong emotions in followers.[18] The empirical literature on charismatic leadership demonstrates that it has profound effects on followers.[19] Modi displayed all the traits of charismatic leadership, which played a critical role in the overall positive effect in his image makeover.

To Be Projected as One Who Can Speak for His Citizens

Certain people asserted that India's incumbent prime minister was shy during public appearances, but these claims were not readily accepted by Indian citizens. Modi wanted to ensure that he would be accepted as an ace orator who could speak for his nation whenever he needed to. Modi has always emphasized his oratory skills by making his words loud, sharp and clear. He orchestrated his speeches with spontaneity, assuring people that his words came straight from his heart. These traits helped Modi connect with the people instantaneously.

Whenever Modi delivers a speech, he stands straight and uses positive body language. His thoughtful posture increases the authenticity of his message, and he comes across as a bold leader of his own words. Modi always uses an appropriate voice tone to ensure that his emotions are expressed in the right manner. By changing the volume and tempo of his voice, stressing keywords such as development, innovation and women's empowerment during his speeches, he shows his passion for these issues.[20]

Modi has made continuous efforts to change his image. He usually tailors his speeches to the audience he is addressing. For instance, when tackling the public at a political rally, he uses common language that appeals to the masses. When speaking at an investor conclave, he uses business-related jargon. In Parliament, he projects himself as a statesman. By using the language he is most comfortable speaking, appropriate body language and effective voice modulation, he has greatly impressed his audiences.[21] Through regionalizing his speeches and using the connotations of local leaders, Modi was an instant hit in India. The Modi wave refers to his capability of connecting with the people of India and acknowledges his dynamism and prowess in leading a nation of 120 crore people.

The concept of charismatic leadership and appealing qualities is explained here:

Charisma is really a process—an interaction between the qualities of the charismatic leader, the followers and their needs and identification with the leader, and the situation that calls out for a charismatic leader, such as a necessity of change or crisis. However, when it comes to the charismatic qualities of leaders, the emphasis is on how they communicate to followers and whether they can gain followers' trust, and influence and persuade them to follow.[22]

To Be Projected as a Leader for the Youth

India has a population of 120 crore people, 65 per cent of whom are youth. Hence it was imperative that Modi was looked at as a leader for the country's young. With almost 2.3 crore first-time voters, the leader who could connect with the youth was expected to have an upper hand in the prime-ministerial race.

While Modi's campaign was largely fought through rallies on the road, a major portion of the campaign was executed through alternative communication channels. Modi used social media to reach out to the youth and made an effort to understand their frustrations and angst.

To connect with the youth, Modi used innovative means of communication, social media, technology and traditional method of mobilization. Twitter, Facebook, Google Hangouts, digital campaigning, 'Chai pe Charcha' in over 4000 locations and 3D rallies covering 1350 sites were all used during his campaign. Modi's campaign coverage on social media was so extensive that he became one of the most popular prime ministers amongst the Indian youth. It is worth noting that even though Modi was sixty-three, the youth considered him as their icon and one amongst them.[23]

To Be Projected as Development Friendly

In the leadership of the previous Congress-led government, India was host to several scams. There was a common perception amongst Indians that their government was not development friendly. It was imperative for Narendra Modi to be portrayed as a minister who would go to any extent to ensure the country's development. Most of his speeches and campaigns referenced the Gujarat growth story to bolster hope among his constituency. His projection as a faithful development minister was a major reason for his victory and is often associated with the so-called Modi wave across India.

Narendra Modi viewed development from a different angle and stressed the three Ss of development: skill, speed and scale. He believed that to make India a global power, matched with the development levels of other countries, work needed to be done on a bigger scale with maximum speed. It had to be done by using the latest technologies and skills effectively.[24]

He not only developed a vision for India's growth, but he also effectively communicated the same through all possible modes of communication, i.e. via rallies, social media and mainstream media. His vision included an eight-point developmental agenda and five essential ingredients of development in the form of five Ts: talent, tourism, transport, tradition and technology.

Sabka Saath Sabka Vikas (Collective Efforts, Inclusive Growth)

India's population of 120 crore includes innumerable castes and religions, and there is widespread discrimination among various factions of the society, along the lines of gender, caste, religion, location, etc. Indian politics is still associated with corruption, bureaucracy and red-tapism. To increase their share of votes, political leaders pit one religion against the other or pit one caste against another. Political leaders have prospered from the votes gained through caste- or religion-based politics for decades. Narendra Modi wanted to ensure that his image was projected as that of an honest leader who treats and respects all men and women equally. Modi's speeches, dialogues and interviews were concentrated on equality rather than discrimination.

India is still referred to as a developing country. Even with a wealth of human and natural resources at India's disposal, the country has not been able to grow at the rate that it could have. One of India's biggest challenges is to achieve inclusive growth, as it is a huge task to bring the 60 crore people living in rural parts of the nation into the mainstream. Attaining growth in all the sections of the society is a major concern.[25]

'Sabka Saath Sabka Vikas' was established to ensure inclusive growth at all levels of Indian society. This mantra urges all sections to unite and 'cooperate' to achieve the country's objectives, instead of working on their individual objectives alone. The programme is based on the idea that betterment and development of society can be reached through 'cooperation' and 'teamwork' between all sections of society.

In a speech Modi said, 'A government has only one style of functioning—*sabka sath sabka vikas*.' He added, 'Let me tell you, I have to run the government. A government runs according to the constitution. I believe that a government has only one religion—India first. A government has only one holy book—our constitution. The government has only one kind of devotion—towards the nation.'[26]

Modi believes that the nation's development, uplift and progress can't be achieved single-handedly, but only through the collective effort of the team as a whole.

Inclusive growth is necessary for sustainable development and fair distribution of wealth. Modi propagated the three-S model for the growth and development of the society. With the motto of collective efforts and inclusive growth, this model accepts and projects urbanization as an opportunity rather than a threat.

Modi linked the three colours of the national flag to three major revolutions that would achieve the overall growth and development of society. Modi defined the Green Revolution, focusing on agro-productivity, value addition, agro-technology and decentralization of warehousing; the White Revolution, focusing on increasing milk productivity and developing a support system for ensuring cattle health; and the Saffron Revolution, focusing on renewable energy sources.[27]

Sadbhavana Mission: Sadbhavana Upvas (Strengthening Social Harmony and Brotherhood)

Indian politics is dominated by blame game, mud-slinging, the poison of caste, the practice of divide and rule and vote-bank politics. All these traits have a negative connotation to them. Narendra Modi ensured his portrayal as a man who believes in unity by strengthening communal harmony and brotherhood. Modi craved to change people's mindsets and wanted to prove to the nation that development and growth can be achieved through social harmony and brotherhood.

Sadbhavana Mission, also known as a Touching People's Movement, was initiated to weigh people's emotional strength, to gauge the bonding between Gujaratis, to represent bonding to the nation and to build communal harmony. The purpose of this mission was to show to the nation that Gujarat's rapid progress was a result of its people's belief in unity, peace and brotherhood.

The main elements of Sadbhavana Mission are:

1. It was held in Ahmedabad from 17–19 September, 2011. Representatives of states and volunteers from other political parties were present.
2. There was a total of thirty-six Sadbhavana fasts that included at least one member from around 70–75 per cent Gujarati families.
3. This mission reflected large-scale public participation, and it included 50 lakh people from 18,000 villages.

External Support Groups

Modi's campaign was powered not only by the BJP's enthusiastic cadre, members of the party, sympathizers of the cause and various party fronts, but also by several groups formed in the past few years in support of Modi or against the UPA government. These groups were not related to the BJP but were largely in support of Modi's candidature for PM and significantly contributed to the elections. In this section, we will look at the groups who mobilized in favour of Modi and how they eventually led to the party's enormous electoral success.

Citizens for Accountable Governance (CAG)

Created in June 2013, CAG was a group of more than 100 like-minded young professionals who came together to bring constructive change in governance and politics. The group was founded by Prashant Kishor, a thirty-six-year-old former UN health specialist, along with five other young professionals—a fresher, an entrepreneur, a lawyer, a software engineer and two investment bankers.

CAG quickly expanded and soon had eight offices all across India with more than 1,04,000 volunteers. CAG claims to be an independent team, working for the PM-elect and not for any political leader or party. CAG identified Modi as a person who could bring accountability in governance. Several key initiatives helped Modi's brand reach and engage directly with millions of Indians with the application of advanced technologies. The initiatives included Samvaad, Manthan, Statue of Unity and Run for Unity, 'Chai pe Charcha', Vijay Sankalp Divas, Moditva, Sankalp, Young Indian Leader Conclave, Modi's 3D rallies and Shreshth Bharat Initiative.

One of the CAG's initial programmes, Manthan, was designed to involve college students in charting the agenda for the 2014 elections. It was an effort to include the aspirations of modern India. Students from over 7000 colleges across India participated and shared innovative solutions to fourteen major issues faced by India today. Teams of five members were organized to work on each of the following fourteen points:

1. Road map for the potential growth of the North-east
2. Universal access to quality primary healthcare

3. Safety and empowerment of women
4. To improve the Public Distribution System and strengthen its reach and efficiency
5. Skill development and the employability of youth
6. Enhancing agricultural productivity
7. Decreasing malnutrition
8. Confirming speedy and timely justice to all
9. Confirming standardized civic amenities for urban class
10. Promoting research and innovation
11. Presenting electoral reforms to minimize the money influence and muscle power in politics
12. Ensuring clean drinking water and appropriate sanitation facility to all
13. Improving the quality of primary education
14. Promoting social welfare of informal sector worker

The students' presentations were first evaluated by a panel of experts and then the shortlisted teams' proposals were voted for online. About 5 lakh students voted online for the shortlisted presentations. Finally, on 2 October 2013, in Thyagaraj Sports Complex, about 7500 students from different parts of the country, the top leadership of the BJP and the Congress party, and other prominent opinion leaders came together to get the ball rolling.

The key purpose of this exercise was to excite young minds and capture their imaginations early on for Modi. There were 18,789 students from more than 700 colleges and 200 cities across India who signed up for Manthan. About 8750 students submitted their ideas, and there were forty-two winning teams in the final rounds. As claimed by CAG, Manthan engaged about one crore students directly and about nine crore youth indirectly through on-ground promotions, college workshops, distribution of publicity material and social media.[28]

Similarly other programmes, such as Samvad, Sankalp, Run for Unity, etc., were largely planned to spread Modi's brand across India, as well as to engage enthusiastic volunteers to work for the party in the coming days. Statue of Unity and Run for Unity galvanized young India, and CAG was able to identify potential volunteers from these programmes. CAG's website claims that more than 48 lakh people ran for this event, the largest number of people to run together in the human history. This event was organized across more than 1050 locations all over India on 15 December 2013, the 63rd death anniversary of Sardar Patel, the Iron Man and the first home minister of India.[29]

This campaign not only mobilized the youth for Modi, but also set the agenda of 'Ek Bharat, Shrestha Bharat [One India, Better India]', i.e. united and integral India, which directly or indirectly targeted the failure of Congress in resolving the issue of J&K and Article 370.

Also, with his mission of 'Congress-mukt Bharat' (Congress-Free India), Modi set the tone for another heated debate, claiming that in Congress only the Gandhi family gets credit no matter their contributions, and Congress had little to defend themselves with in this case.

Chai Pe Charcha

'I promise you, in 21st Century Narendra Modi will never become the Prime Minister of the country . . . But if he wants to distribute tea here, we will find a place for him,' said Mani Shankar Aiyar at the venue of the All India Congress Committee (AICC) meeting in Delhi on 18 January 2014.[30]

When Mani Shankar Aiyar said this, he may not have imagined that he was giving Modi a weapon to mobilize India around. Modi not only capitalized on this statement by attacking the 'Ruler' mentality of Congress but also translated it into a personal attack by relating it to his experience as a tea seller. The already polarized Modi enthusiasts were emotionally disturbed and further antagonized by Congress.

Team BJP and CAG immediately saw an opportunity to build a campaign around this theme and came up with the much talked about 'Chai Pe Charcha' programme. They utilized advanced technology to conduct these programmes simultaneously at hundreds of places, and via video conferencing Modi reached millions.

The first such programme was held on 12 February 2014, within a month of Aiyar's remark. From Iskcon Gandhi tea stall in western Ahmedabad, Modi connected electronically with lakhs of his supporters and curious onlookers. The event was aired live at 1000 places across 300 cities. Locations and timings were selected in a way to maximize footfall. Such 'Chai Pe Charcha' programmes/stalls were also organized on the sides of a few busy highways to attract commuters and tourists. Even in this, Modi addressed the issue of good governance. The mode of this event allowed participants to ask questions directly to Modi. The next 'Chai Pe Charcha' was focused on women's empowerment and was organized at more than 1500 locations in over 500 cities.[31] In these discussions, Modi effectively touched on the difficulties faced by a woman in her daily life and pledged to help them transform from a 'homemaker' to a 'nation builder'.

The third and last round of 'Chai Pe Charcha' focused on 'Farmers and Agrarian Crisis'. It was especially dedicated to the farmers of Maharashtra, who have faced continuous crises and several of them have been forced to take extreme steps due to government apathy. This event was organized in the Dhabhadi village of Yavatmal district of Maharashtra, where many farmers were devastated by an unusual hailstorm that had destroyed acres of crops.

During this event, Modi interacted directly with the farmers from Maharashtra, Karnataka, Andhra Pradesh, West Bengal, Bihar, Odisha, Uttar Pradesh, Punjab, Himachal Pradesh, Madhya Pradesh and other places.

The discussion was also organized at 281 locations in Uttar Pradesh, where he interacted with farmers and discussed their issues. Smaller versions of 'Chai pe Charcha' were also arranged as per the needs of specific parliamentary constituencies.

Each of these three events was effectively and efficiently planned in its choice of day, place and the issue to be discussed so that it could reach the maximum amount of people. This innovative concept was a hit not only on social media, but also in the national and international media. It is estimated that via these 'Chai pe Charcha' events, Modi interacted with 2 crore people across more than 4000 national and international locations.[32]

This initiative had far-reaching advantages and its efficacy can be understood in the light of research evidence.[33] Use of tea and the tea stalls may be considered in emotional context to be conceptual priming. Priming means providing a stimulus to the human mind that can influence our future thoughts and actions. In other words, when an individual is exposed to a stimulus (tea in this case) it can increase recall between an associated person and the stimulus and also increase the meaning ascribed to the object that is influenced by the stimulus.

Thus, tea (arguably India's national drink) may have a priming effect on the candidate attached to tea in two ways. First, sight or mention of tea will aid recall about the candidate concerned. Second, tea (seen as a national drink, a simple drink, an affordable drink, everyone's drink and a refreshing drink) can have a similar priming effect on the candidate. Hence, 'Chai pe Charcha' does not remind voters of BJP or local candidates but reminds them of a positive image of Narendra Modi.

3D Rallies

Modi had no competitors in his use of technology to increase outreach and force the mainstream media to pay attention. Despite spending Rs 500 crore on a massive advertisement campaign, Congress Vice President Rahul Gandhi struggled to make a mark. Modi has been India's most tech-savvy politician. He seems to have surpassed Barack Obama, whose presidential 2009 election campaign was touted as being the most tech-savvy so far.

Modi was the first to use such technology for mass outreach. He first used this technology during the November 2012 Gujarat elections. During the 2012 Gujarat assembly election, NChant 3D broadcast Modi's speech to around fifty-three locations across twenty-six cities in Gujarat. During the assembly elections, Modi addressed about 200 public meetings using this technology. The technology not only enabled the BJP team to simultaneously reach out to voters in various constituencies, but also minimized security threats.

During his 2014 election campaign, Modi addressed 1350 rallies with this technology, 600 of which were planned during the last lap of the elections.[34] While, Modi's persona attracted people to these rallies, many voters of different ages wanted to experience the technology.

Other CAG Initiatives

Several other initiatives were taken to strengthen Modi's brand and extend its reach.

1. *Moditva: The Idea behind the Man*
    A book compiling Modi's vision and philosophy that includes fourteen essays discussing the Modi model of governance.
2. Samvaad
    A movement focused on agrarian distress in India. Samvaad was planned to warn the nation of the severity of the problem through large-scale, informed and continuous engagement. It organized the world's largest petition to the Government of India, demanding decisive action towards farmer suicides in the country.
3. The Indian Republic
    A news portal designed to spread messages to an online audience.
4. Shreshtha Bharat
    A joint initiative of Lodha Foundation, Shahid Gaurav Samiti and CAG aimed at reinstalling a sense of patriotism. With events such as 'Saluting the Defence Forces of India', 'Ae Mere Watan Ke Logon' and 'Zara Yaad Karo Kurbani', a patriotic flavour was given to the elections. Lata Mangeshkar was felicitated by Modi at the golden jubilee year of her song 'Ae mere watan ke logon'

on 27 January 2014 as part of Shreshtha Bharat Divas celebrations.

5. Sankalp

This initiative aimed to raise awareness about existing gender disparity in India, crimes against women and to lessen the gap between the launch of women-related policies and their implementation. Essentially, this was targeted at reaching out to 50 per cent of the voting population.

6. Manthan

As discussed earlier, this was a youth conference tasked with setting up the agenda for the general elections of 2014.

7. iVote

An attempt to inspire bigger participation by the younger generation in the electoral process. As per the CAG website, it aimed to:

- Bring together youth from all over the country who believe in the cause of involving larger number of youth in the electoral process.
- Empower these youth to conduct awareness and voter registration drives through digital media and at colleges, workplaces and neighborhoods.
- Recognize and reward the efforts of these youth by promoting them as champions of the bigger cause through online and on-ground (national, state and citywide) events.

8. Young Indian Leader Conclave

About 200 young leaders attended this conference to discuss India Vision 2020. It aimed to discuss how better employment opportunities could be given to the young generation of India and the necessary government initiatives. The forum was addressed by Modi and former President of India A.P.J. Abdul Kalam.

9. Modi Aane Vala Hai

'Modi Aane Vala Hai' was one of the campaign songs of BJP. Sung by famous Bollywood singer Udit Narayan, it was released during the BJP National Executive Council meet on 19 January 2014. The song portrays a larger-than-life image of Modi. Akhil Bharatiya Vidyarthi Parishad (ABVP), the student wing of RSS, and CAG jointly took responsibility for bringing this song to the people living in the remotest areas of the country. A small vehicle decorated with the saffron colour, pictures of Atal Bihari Vajpayee and Narendra Modi, and a 55" LCD screen carried the message of Modi and party president Rajnath Singh by playing the song. Each vehicle also carried an inverter, an amplifier and a DVD player. A telephone number was prominently displayed, enabling people to connect to Modi with a missed call.

The event planned to cover all 403 assembly seats across the state of Uttar Pradesh (UP), focusing on 19,000 villages; particularly those in inaccessible areas where cavalcades of senior leaders could not venture and television sets were rare. The vehicles also carried the electoral rolls of the areas falling along its route, as well as pamphlets and masks of Modi. Four hundred such vehicles were used to cover all the parliamentary constituencies in UP. The event was planned meticulously, taking each election phase into consideration. Vehicles were closely monitored via GPS. Location of any vehicle and the name of its driver were readily available to the control room in Lucknow.

10. Vijay Sankalp Divas

This was jointly conducted by BJP and CAG on 6 April 2014, BJP's 34th foundation day. Incidentally, this was just one day before phase one of the elections. A key objective of this event was pan-India mobilization of party workers. Along with celebrations of the foundation of BJP, booth-level cadres pledged to work for the party's electoral victory and to reach households in their respective areas. Booth-level cadres were expected to discuss the following points with the voters:

- Why the country needs Modi as the prime minister.
- Provide information about the local candidate and the election symbol of the lotus.
- Request voters to give a missed call to a designated number, to capture their details in the party's database for future use and as an indicator of support.

During this outreach programme, female party workers drew the symbolic lotus with henna on their hands, attracting and engaging women voters. The event covered more than 400 parliamentary constituencies, 6 lakh polling booths and 2–3 crore voters. Using technology, the party's booth-level cadres were directly put in touch with Modi and party's senior leadership team. This helped the party prepare and galvanize the cadre, a day before the beginning of the elections.

NaMo Brigade

Launched in 2014, this brigade of young and passionate youth including professionals, young entrepreneurs, self-employed people and college students wished to bring political change by ousting the current corrupt and non-performing UPA government. The group included members who were staunch supporters of Modi and wished to see him as the prime minister . The sole objective of the group was to focus on the 2014 parliamentary elections and to mobilize as many youth as possible in the electoral process.

After the launch of their NaMo Brigade website, more than 7000 like-minded youth registered for this initiative. Another 3 lakh volunteers showed their support by giving a missed call to a specified number arranged by the brigade. For visible impact, the brigade released merchandise such as T-shirts, labels, badges, etc. Soon the brigade spread their message to more than 140 assembly constituencies in Karnataka, creating substantial mobilization for Modi.

After their great success in Karnataka, the programme was again launched in Mumbai. The brigade focused on one key objective: registering more and more youth on the electoral list. To achieve this, the brigade organized workshops for all chapter coordinators. Training was given to volunteers on how to best spread Modi's message across the state, how to register voters and how to ensure that people received their voter ID cards on time.

With a presence in two states, and in almost all parliamentary constituencies of Karnataka, this syndicate was a force of more than 20,000 volunteers. These volunteers reached more than 15 lakh voters. It was a big push in the state of Karnataka, where prospects of electoral success of BJP were thin after they badly lost assembly polls in May 2013.

They organized various events and shows to mobilize support for Modi, including bike rallies wearing 'Modi'fied T-shirts. The brigade organized 'NaMo Bharat' musical concert for selling Modi's brand in the gateway of south India for the BJP. The show focused largely on the achievements of Modi as the CM of Gujarat and his vision for India. Innovative initiatives such as NaMo SunoCaller Tunes, NaMo Radio Station, NaMo Anthem and NaMo Namah were undertaken to take Modi's brand and his development agenda to the masses. A creative mix of songs, caller tunes and storytelling were used to catch the attention of the common man. The brigade regularly organized silent campaigns at crowded places such as malls and railway stations on weekends. Wankhede Stadium, Mumbai, where Sachin played his last innings, also became a venue for the promotion of the NaMo Brigade. It also regularly utilized the traditional billboards and hoardings to spread the message. Huge billboards and posters on vehicles grabbed the attention of passers-by. The brigade also developed the NaMo Android apps and used Facebook extensively to share information and mobilize opinion.

NaMoleague

This platform focused on development projects in Gujarat, specifically the leadership of Narendra Modi in planning and executing various visionary projects in the state. They organized programmes such as 'Write for NaMo' in which thousands of people wrote slogans for Narendra Modi. This team worked in collaboration with NaMo Mantra, a NaMo merchandise brand. They distributed NaMo Mantra merchandise to the winners of the competition.

Narendra Modi Vichar Manch

This platform was created in Kannur, Kerala, by some discontent party workers, who were then pressing for the declaration of Modi's candidature for PM. Formed in October 2013, this platform took the shape of an NGO serving needy and socially backward people, providing them medical facilities and teaching them lessons of good conduct, society and nation. Simultaneously, they kept on mobilizing opinion for Modi as PM candidate.

Mission Protect India (MPI)[35]

MPI was an initiative by some ardent Modi fans who thought that only Modi could save this country from the crisis it was facing because of the current UPA government. This attitude is reflected in their slogan 'Modi Lao, Desh Bachao'. The group was formed by eminent social activists and spiritual guru Rajbir Singh Dhaka.

This mission started with the idea of reforming India by observing the current scenario and the political behaviours of those who are considered responsible. The next step was to spread awareness among the general public about the necessity for change. They started their work in early 2013.

During an interview one of the office-bearers mentioned that their support for Modi was not just based on the 'good work Modi Ji did, but for astrological reasons as well. With the help of numerology it was found that Modi would not only be the most capable and suitable person to lead the country out of the turmoil but also he was destined to become the PM.' Hence, they formed the group and started educating the masses via activities, both on and off the ground. MPI carried out several programmes and events in support of Modi. They organized Modi's Sadbhavana Yatra anniversary in December 2013 to show their support for NaMo as PM. They organized a Sadbhavana Yatra starting from Ajmer Sharif to the temple of Lord Brahma in Pushkar, Rajasthan. They conducted a padyatra from Delhi to Faridabad (Haryana) and organized a motorcycle rally in Varanasi in support of Modi. They conveyed their message to the BJP during the Dharm Sansad organized by Vishva Hindu Parishad (VHP) in Allahabad. Later, they organized regular protests and demonstrations during the BJP's national executive meetings and National Council Meetings to put forward their points. MPI wrote to 325 national leaders of the BJP, requesting them to extend their support to Modi's candidature. During elections, MPI members extended huge support in bringing people to Modi's rallies.

Branding Gujarat and the Halo Effect

Modi worked relentlessly to promote the state of Gujarat, not just in India but also across the globe. He roped in Bollywood icon Amitabh Bachchan as the brand ambassador of Gujarat. The underlying idea was to promote places such as Kutch, Dwarka, etc., that exhibit a rich Indian cultural heritage. Getting Amitabh Bachchan as the brand ambassador was a master stroke, since he has a huge fan following across the globe. This resulted in an effective promotional campaign for Gujarat.[36] Gujarat had only one hill station—Saputara. Hence it became even more necessary to ensure that effective marketing strategies were in place to promote Saputara as a tourist attraction. The hill station is located in the Sahyadri Hills, and it enjoys a pleasant and cool climate. Promoting Saputara as a favoured tourist attraction called for big investments to build the necessary infrastructural facilities. As expected, there has been a notable spike in Gujarat Tourism index ever since Modi and Saurabh Patel

(Gujarat tourism minister at the time of campaign) anchored these aggressive promotional campaigns. Credit also goes to Bachchan who, with his huge fan following, helped position Gujarat as a state with diverse offerings to tourists of all interests.

Kutch, Dwarka, Somnath and Gir Forest National Park—areas that were all part of Bachchan's campaign— have experienced a 30 per cent increase in foreign tourists. The rising popularity of Gujarat as an attractive tourist place catapulted the state to the 5th spot on India's tourism index. (Rajasthan, Kerala, Maharashtra and Goa were the four states ahead of Gujarat.) The state has a rich Buddhist heritage which takes the form of rock-cut caves across Sabarkantha, Vadnagar, Junagadh, Rajkot, Kutch and Bharuch. Despite the fact that Gujaratis love to travel, the Gujarat tourism industry never took off. Thanks to Modi and Patel's concerted efforts towards promotion of Gujarati tourism, the inflow of tourists has dramatically increased over the years. From 1.2 lakh in 2006–07, the number grew by almost 42 per cent to 1.7 lakh in 2009–10 to over 2 lakh in 2010–11. The period between May–September 2011 experienced 13 lakh more tourists than the same months during the previous year. Gujarat's government also roped in known adman Piyush Pandey to create advertisements that promoted Gujarat Tourism. The ad campaign comprised of three short films, each sixty seconds long and centred on the ethereal beauty of Kutch, the sanctity of pilgrimage places such as the Somnath temple and the picturesque landscape and wildlife of the Gir Forest. Such an aggressive tourism campaign was the first of its kind for the state of Gujarat in particular and was the brainchild of Narendra Modi. The result was effective; more than 1000 visitors flocked to Gir

Forest in a day. According to Sandeep Kumar, the deputy conservator of Gir National Park, this number had never been seen before.

To keep a close tab on illegal activities such as poaching, entry into the sanctuary has been highly restricted since 2000—a move initiated in the interest of wildlife conservation. Initially, only around ninety vehicles were permitted inside. Due to an increase in demand, this number was increased to 150. Safety measures were tightened so that there was no illegal activity. The national park greatly benefited financially. Thanks to the increased tourist activity, the national park recorded an all-time high revenue of over Rs 45 lakh in the first fortnight of November 2010[37]. This is in comparison to a revenue of Rs 2.10 crore in the eight months between October and May (2009–10) when the monthly average was a paltry Rs 26 lakh.

A similar positive effect was observed during 'Rann Utsav', which takes place in the month of December in the Kutch district. Every year, the festival takes place over three days and witnesses visitors from across the country. Keeping in line with the increasing popularity of Gujarat as a tourist destination, in 2007 the government decided to extend the celebrations for a month so that it would include New Year's and uttarayan (Makar Sankranti) as well.

The tourism corporation also sought the approval of the director general of civil aviation (DGCA) to commence a chopper service during the festival. This initiative was well received by visitors because it made travelling quicker and more comfortable. Also, thanks to the air service, tourists could now cover multiple places within a short period of time, adding to the revenue stream of the Gujarat Tourism Corporation.[38]

Managing Workforce in Action: AAP's Delhi Election

Team of the 'Uncommon'

The majority of AAP team members have the same agenda and a unanimous objective. It is a diverse group, and many of its members have overcome many setbacks in their personal and professional lives. They took a calculated risk to enter politics for a clean and corruption-free India. The AAP is comprised of professionals, poets, tech-savvy people and journalists.

Kumar Vishwas, a popular poet among the youth, along with Punjab MP Bhagwant Mann, a comedian turned politician, and former actress and bike rider Gul Panag added flavour to the campaign, helping to bring in large crowds. These campaigns, along with the presence of formidable public figures, had a beneficial effect on the party's grand march to a historic win. The message that candidates were common people created the magic for AAP. This win proved that money is not the only part of winning elections in India.

One can always learn from the leaders and people who have applied and tested the success formula. It is quite evident from the BJP's victory that face of election campaigning has changed because new issues have emerged. Caste, religion and class can no longer be the main agendas for fighting elections. People want development, and they want to ensure that their future is secure. Kejriwal, like a smart bania (member of the business community), learned the trade art from Modi and immediately applied it in assembly elections.

5

EFFECTIVE MEDIA USAGE

Internet and mobile phones are ubiquitous, and social media has become a mainstay of the politically inclined. Social media has a significant impact on the lifestyles and perceptions of consumers, as well as those of the masses. Online word of mouth (WOM) has become central to the younger population and has a large influence on their decision-making. However, when trying to analyse the content of WOM discourses, it is difficult to identify the correct metrics to gauge its essence. A number of algorithms have been developed to track changes in WOM online. This system was heavily used in the general election of 2014 by the BJP's IT cell, and it was also adopted by AAP in Delhi assembly elections of 2015.

A more recent study of interpersonal communication concerning 'products' suggests that 'people have altered the level of abstraction in their messages during interpersonal communication about "others"'.[1] Systematic variations in language also significantly affect the message's recipients.[2]

Personalization of Prime Ministers/Chief Ministers in India

The elections for the coveted posts of prime minister or chief minister (over the years the candidate for PM's post or CM's post has belonged to a party with national presence) are seen as the heart of our political system. A candidate is viewed as the flamboyant face of democracy—a liberator, defender and saviour. Scholars supported this idea when they evaluated candidates on their abilities with 'public communication', 'policy vision' and 'cognitive skills'.[3] In these scenarios, the media also portrays candidates as active and concerned, or as people who can govern the country in an altruistic manner.

This campaigner's attitude that 'I-am-bigger-than-the-party' originated in the Nehruvian era of election campaigning though there were no other options available. In 1947, Jawaharlal Nehru became the first prime minister of Independent India. Nehru was the obvious choice for the PM's post, supported by M.K. Gandhi. At that point of time, Congress was the major party with all the firebrand politicians. According to Congress Working Committee (CWC), elected president of congress would become the first prime minister of India. This was decided in the interim election of 1946 in which Congress won the maximum seats. Nehru, after becoming the PM, was the most beloved politician of the country. He had achieved this through his charming personality and socialist approach of nation-building. His closest competitor for PM's post, Sardar Vallabhbhai Patel, died in 1950. M.K. Gandhi died in 1948. Eventually, Nehru was the only politician left to lead the nation. He remained the PM of India till 1964. This Nehruvian era of election campaigning continued into Indira Gandhi's political career and influenced the first coalition government of the BJP and allies under Atal Bihari Vajpayee ('Abki Bari Atal Bihari') for 13 days in 1996 and from 1998 to 2004. Congress ruled over the country for almost sixty years after Independence as sole decision makers. After Congress's descent, Sonia Gandhi, wife of former prime minister Rajiv Gandhi, became the cynosure. She single-handedly made decisions for the party, probably on behalf of the ruling government.

For once, it was evident that every minister or ministry in India required her 'go-ahead' before they could implement any policy. One could say that our political system is inescapably fascinated with these larger-than-life figures. The three stalwarts of the Nehru–Gandhi family, who captured the office post-Independence, were tagged on virtually every building, scheme, hospital, road, airport and important office across the country. Around ninety-eight universities and educational institutions, nineteen stadiums, twenty-eight tournaments, fifteen scholarships and five airports and ports bear the name of one of these three politicians.[4]

In 1996, when the NDA, a coalition government of the BJP and their allies, came into power, Atal Bihari Vajpayee was the face of the campaign. Due to the slogan 'Abki Bari Atal Bihari',[5] for the first time, the BJP won a significant amount of seats across the country. For the first time, Vajpayee was delighted by the media's support of his style, personality, ability and image. Voters saw Vajpayee so favourably that they voted for him, not for the BJP. He possessed the image of a clean and honest politician who could make 'India Shine'.

There are many parallels between Indian politicians' larger-than-life, almost god-like images and the common perception of US presidential candidates as 'redeemers'. Presidential candidates are seen as warriors who can fly fighter planes to rescue their fellow citizens from alien attacks and single-handedly take on terrorists. It is almost like the American superheroes who are depicted as saviours in crisis. They are known for their heroism and patriotism. Presidential candidates are 'exceptional' figures indeed. Despite being bound by constitutional law, they are still portrayed as single executors.

The great mountain of Rushmore in the United States is sculpted to depict images of the four most revered US Presidents—George Washington, Thomas Jefferson, Abraham Lincoln and Theodore Roosevelt. This reveals the god-like image Americans hold of these noble men, who do not have the flaws of other countrymen. Over the years, successors of these 'gods' have tried to put themselves in the same shoes, attempting to exemplify them in their speech and deeds. History shows records of impeachment against Presidents Richard Nixon and Bill Clinton, yet they are still revered and worshipped as idols. Nixon was seen at times as orthodox in his policies. According to a document by Miller Center of Public Affairs, his most creditable achievements as a President were the nuclear arms agreement with the erstwhile Soviet Union and the development of diplomatic relationship with China. These two important diplomatic decisions brought an end to the Cold War. His involvement in the Watergate cover-up and his conviction to prolong Vietnam War until his re-election resulted in his exit from the White House.[6] As Rauch[7] argued, 'Nixon's secret bombings, his wartime lies, his betrayal of the voters all taught millions of Americans that government could not be trusted.' Probably this fuelled scepticism in the entire generation about politicians and decisions of presidency. He was the only President ever to have resigned from the office. Ultimately, presidential power relies on Congress's actions.[8] The President has the executive power to implement laws, but Congress can still overrule such orders. Congress gives certain powers to the President, but they can be curtailed or withdrawn whenever the party wishes to do so.

Narendra Modi's movement in Gujarat can be analysed in a similar way. Modi's journey from being a simple pracharak (volunteer in RSS) to becoming the chief minister of the state can be attributed to his strategic crafting of an 'I-am-bigger-than-my-party' image. He changed the rules of the game, and within ten years became the centre of attention. His popularity as a successful leader and a promising politician was so strong that even party stalwarts could not deny his prime-ministerial candidacy.

Politicians' image personalization creates a dilemma between different political positions and competency. When this dilemma persists over the years in political philosophy, it is difficult to determine whether an individual party member or the collective strength of the party has more power. The Gujarat government's progress model has been examined in terms of its various programmes, policies and strategies. It was found that though many of Gujarat's programmes were proposed by the government under the constitutional laws and regime, most of them were referred to as 'Modi Ideas'.

Modi was very clear that his agenda was to transform Gujarat into a developed state by creating a stable and sustainable environment for businesses to grow. In the line of action, he made several bold decisions, like pushing for changes in the age-old laws, single-window clearance for businesses, implementing women and child development schemes and extensively promoting tourism. Though these were all implemented through the collective action of the state government, they were largely marketed as Modi's ideas. Development in Gujarat has been continuously attributed to the strong leadership and determination of Modi.

'Vibrant Gujarat' initially started as an investor summit to promote opportunities in the state for investments and businesses. Seven years later, it became a brand. The 'Vibrant Gujarat' programme was the Gujarat government's flagship plan to convince investors from across the globe to participate in this one-of-a-kind Indian initiative. The event has been marketed as a 'brainchild of Modi'.

Other states such as Madhya Pradesh, Rajasthan and West Bengal have adopted this same strategy, but 'Vibrant Gujarat' is still seen as Modi's model of development and promotion. After assuming office as the prime minister of India, Modi changed the country's foreign policy towards neighbouring countries and developed nations. Modi was praised for his consecutive visits to the US, Japan and Australia. The media diverted all its attention towards Modi's strategy of negotiations with foreign counterparts rather than focusing on foreign policy. The entire scenario is seen as 'Modi magic' in the US, Japan and the other countries he visited.

The above discussion emphasizes the personalization of an individual like the prime minister or the chief of the states, making the position individualistic. Even if the office-bearer is an influential leader, decisions cannot be personalized. Acknowledging one person instead of an entire team is unjust because it is not an individual's work but the combined effort of numerous government members to propose ideas and implement decisions in the governing and development of the country. Government members need to be appreciated to motivate them, which is beneficial in the long run for the ruling party and country's development.

Vibrant Campaign Connected with Every Caste and Class

Communication in Action: The Case of Social Media Campaign

Campaign activities are crucial for any party, especially when one is contesting elections. It is required not only to create mega campaigns or mass campaigns, but also to ensure public support. A campaign without public support is like a megastar movie without viewers. For a successful outcome, a campaign's objectives as well as its duration, budget and the involvement of party workers are all crucial. Obama's 2008 US presidential campaign was entirely novel. The campaign used social media as a medium for public engagement, accurately targeting an already dedicated audience as well as potential supporters. It encouraged voters to go to the polling booths. The initiative was well planned and strategically applied.

The BJP successfully used the mantra 'Modi is the face of BJP' in the general elections. Party workers were responsible for disseminating this message across the entire country. All activities were planned so that Modi remained at the centre of the stage, though people still voted for the BJP as a party.

In previous elections, reaching each and every voter in a constituency was challenging. In some cases, candidates rallied around the major areas of their constituency once or twice. This probably had a limited impact, but technological advancements and easy access through mobile phones and Internet connection allowed people to connect to each other. These days campaign activity has to be planned so that voters are dragged to popular platforms for discussions, sharing and one-on-one dialogue. In political campaigning it takes time to target voters. One must develop a persuasive message and then contact voters directly. A written campaign plan is like the preliminary plan for building a house: it defines the overall political landscape, strategy and resources required to get to election day.

While it is true that every campaign is unique, some basic principles can be applied to them all. The basics of any election campaign are relatively straightforward. All campaigns must repeatedly communicate a persuasive message to the people who will vote. This is 'the golden rule' of politics. A political campaign is a communication process whereby one finds the right message, targets that message to the right group of voters and then conveys the message repeatedly.

Yet there is much more that goes into the process of campaign planning. Here are some suggested steps for a political campaign:[9]

1.   Doing the necessary research work to prepare for the campaign:

     •   What is the type of election and what are the rules?
     •   What are the characteristics of the district?
     •   What are the characteristics of the voters?
     •   What has happened in previous elections?
     •   What are the main factors affecting this election?
     •   What are the strengths and weaknesses of your candidate?
     •   What are the strengths and weaknesses of all the viable opponents?

2.   Setting a strategic campaign goal to determine how many votes are needed to win:

     •   How many people (not just voters) live in your district?
     •   How many of these people can vote in this election?

- What percentage of these voters do you expect to vote in this election?
- How many expected voters is this in real numbers?
- How many candidates will be running for this position?
- How many of these candidates could be considered serious?
- If the election were held today, what percentage of the vote do you think each candidate would receive?
- What percentage of the votes cast is needed to win?
- How many votes cast in real numbers are needed to win?
- On an average, how many voters live in one household?
- Do all the voters living in the same household tend to vote for the same candidate?
- If they do tend to vote for the same candidate, how many households will you need to receive a guaranteed victory?
- If you talk to ten average voters, how many of them can you persuade to vote for you?
- How many households will you need to communicate your message to, so that the necessary number of voters is influenced to achieve victory?

3. Analysing and targeting voters:
   Geographic targeting:

- Where do all the candidates live? Are there any distinct geographic areas of support for any particular candidate?
- What are the past performances of similar candidates in each precinct of the district?

- How persuadable are voters in each precinct of the district?
- What is the expected turnout of each precinct of the district?

Demographic targeting:

- What are the demographic profiles (age, gender, profession, education, etc.) of all the viable candidates, including your candidate?
- What demographic groups should support your candidate?
- Are there enough votes within these groups to win the election?
- Where do these demographic groups gather? How do they get their information?
- Are there other candidates appealing to the same demographic groups?
- What demographic groups will you concede to your opponents?
- What collateral groups might you appeal to if needed?

Bringing together all the target voters:

- List all the likely supporters, both geographically and demographically.
- List all the potential supporters, both geographically and demographically.
- List all the unlikely supporters that you will concede to your opponents.
- What are the values of both likely and potential supporters? Do they differ in any significant way?

- What are their attitudes?
- What issues concern these voters?
- What leadership qualities are they looking for?

Developing a campaign message:

- What do voters care about, and how do they get their information?
- What is the message?
- Is the message credible, truthful, clear and persuasive?
- Is this message targeted?
- Why are you running for this office?

Developing a voter contact plan:

- The rule of finite resources: It is critical to remember that you have only a finite resource.
- Identify the voter contact activities.
- Identify the effectiveness of your voter contact activities.

Implementing that plan:

- Making a proper schedule for contacts, persuasion and fundraising.
- Coordinating with different members of the team.
- Leaving room for midway course correction.

Post his resignation from chief minister's post in Delhi, Arvind Kejriwal was heavily criticized. The AAP was aware of the consequences of not delivering on the promises they had relied on to gain the trust of Delhi citizens, and it was a risk

Voter Contact Tasks	Effectiveness				Resources	
	Persuade Voters	Identify Supporters	Turn out Vote	Time	Money	People
Literature Drop	Yes	No	Yes	Yes		Yes
Literature Handouts	Maybe	No	Maybe			Yes
Mail	Yes	No	Yes		Yes	
Door to Door	Yes	Yes	No	Yes		Yes
Phoning	Maybe	Yes	Yes	Yes	Yes	Yes
Visibility	No	No	Yes	Yes	Yes	Yes
Endorsements	Yes	Maybe	Maybe	Yes		Yes
Coffee	Yes	Yes	No	Yes		Yes
Dear Friends	Yes	No	Yes	Yes		Yes
Present Events	Maybe	Maybe	No	Yes		Yes
Created Events	Maybe	No	Maybe	Yes	Yes	Yes
Press	Yes	No	Maybe	Yes	Yes	Yes
Advertisements	Yes	No	Yes		Yes	
Web	Maybe	No	No		Yes	

Source: O'Day, J. Brian, *Political Campaign Planning Manual, a Step by Step Guide to Winning Elections*[10]

to contest in elections on national level before fulfilling their commitments to the regional public. The Modi wave and the spectral game of BJP swept the AAP's mission. It was a time for serious introspection. BJP and Modi were the first choice for voters across the country. While analyzing various articles and election proceedings, it was pretty clear that voters wanted to see BJP in the Centre under Modi's leadership. People were aware of the good work that Modi had done in Gujarat. The same development and good work was expected from him at the Centre.

For the second time, the AAP showed that it did not need a long runway to take off. What gave the party a lift was its massive army of dedicated workers and volunteers who were always on the ground. In 2013, the party made a stellar electoral debut, with the Delhi assembly elections, although it did not join the race till September. This time it did not galvanize till December of 2014, but after that it did not lose its focus and applied a radical and different strategy altogether. Though they formally started rallies and jan sabhas on 1 December, their team had been involved in an intensive door-to-door (what we call 'man-to-man marketing') campaign.

The VS–JS Model: 'Vidhan Sabha–Jan Sabha Model'

This was one of the most effective parts of their campaigning process. AAP stuck to its VS–JS focus on small areas and organized only one big road show, as compared to the mega rallies frequently organized by the BJP and Congress. The AAP consulted the people of Delhi to prepare its manifesto in a series of discussions revolving around water, power, women's safety, Swaraj, Jan Lokpal, education and health; calling it 'The Delhi Dialogue'. These involved residents, policymakers and experts looking for solutions to common problems. Decisions from the dialogues were merged to make the party manifesto. This was one of the key characteristics of AAP 3.0 campaigning, with its 'positive agenda', marking a change of style from the 'mud-slinging' that other parties normally used to discredit their opponents.

'Mission Vistaar'

The National Executive of the Aam Aadmi Party developed an initiative called 'Mission Vistaar' in June of 2014. The initiative was aimed at expanding and restructuring the AAP, at multistage levels. The main agendas of the initiative were to:

1. Reach out to the many citizens of this country who share the ideology of the Aam Aadmi Party and want to play a meaningful role in nation-building.
2. Integrate all these change makers into the party organization by providing opportunities for them to take up responsibilities within the party.
3. Evolve a meaningful and effective two-way communication system among volunteers and between various levels of party organization.
4. Facilitate the process of political education and leadership building amongst those who have joined the Aam Aadmi Party, making them catalysts of change in the country.
5. Reorganize the organizational units at various levels through a bottom-up democratic process.[11]

The party appointed observers to supervise its process of reformation and expansion at every stage. The observers started travelling throughout the state to organize meetings with candidates, volunteers, party members and committees at district levels. After collecting feedback, their role was to analyse the performances of various state units at the time of the general elections. The State Mission Vistaar Committee was then tasked with developing the party into a strong organization, keeping its time-bound restructuring synchronized with performance targets. The State Mission Vistaar Committee appointed interim district Mission Vistaar committees after consulting with district volunteers.

Goal Setting for Volunteers

- Development of the party at booth level.
- Recruitment of at least two dedicated volunteers and as many members as possible at the polling booth.
- All the activities of volunteers were prudently traced and verified.
- Volunteers were asked to choose activities that could be conducted for local voters. For example, helping people with issues such as RTI, right to education (RTE) and access to the Public Distribution System, examining voter lists in door-to-door visits, and disseminating information within the allocated budget.

Bottom-to-Top Democratic Organization Structure

As per the party's constitution, active members would be given the opportunity to participate in elections and be considered as voters and/or candidates to achieve a democratically elected party. This was attempted in a bottom-to-top democratic process to elect governing bodies and party committees at different levels. The overarching goal of Mission Vistaar was to expand and to extend the reach of the party organization while keeping in line with the party's constitutional principles of transparency and intra-party democracy.

One of the first things that Arvind Kejriwal did after the Delhi elections was reflect on his mistakes. He did something very uncommon in Indian politics—he apologized to the people of Delhi for leaving the CM's post after forty-nine days. This initiative was relatively well-received by voters, and he appeared to be sincere and human. At the same time, this gesture snatched away the Opposition's opportunity to call him a deserter.

Organizational Restructuring

After the general elections in 2014, there was consensus within the party on the necessity of organizational restructuring. The party also realized that they had overstretched their one-year-old party's resources by contesting over 400 seats nationwide and that they needed to return their focus to Delhi.

At the organizational level, the AAP realized that one person could not manage everything, and the structure had to be reframed. The party needed to build a new bridge to reach out to voters who had moved away. In order to get back their accountability, they switched to a clear system to divide responsibility, and individuals were put in charge of districts. 'The onus of winning these districts was with the individual,' said Durgesh Pathak, part of the Delhi Election Campaign Group, in an interview to the *Indian Express*.[12]

| National Convener |
| Arvind Kejriwal |

| Political Affairs Committee | Election Campaign Group |
| Gopal Rai, Manish Sisodia, Pankaj Gupta, Kumar Vishwas, Prashant Bhushan, Yogendra Yadav, Iliyas Azmi, Sanjay Singh | Arvind Kejriwal, Manish Sisodia, Gopal Rai, Pankaj Gupta, Ashutosh, Dileep Pandey, Durgesh Pathak, Ashish Talwar, Rakesh Sinha, Rishikesh Kumar, Richa Mishra Pandey, Nagendra Sharma, Deepak Bajpai, Ashish Khetan |

The party appointed fourteen district supervisors, each responsible for five assembly constituencies. One of the criteria for district supervisors was that they had to have been with the party for over a year and a half. Many were former campaign managers, and two of these fourteen, Praveen Deshmukh and Nitin Tyagi, went on to become candidates and eventually MLAs.

Every alternate day, at 8.30 a.m., these fourteen district supervisors would interact in a conference call. They were the real heroes of the campaign. Their responsibilities were to build the organization and volunteer-base in their area, give input for the candidate-selection process and implement the party's campaign. Two members of the party's central leadership, Durgesh Pathak and Dilip Pandey, were responsible for presiding over the meetings of seven districts. Once a week, all sixteen of them would meet the party's national convener Arvind Kejriwal in a 'review meeting' to exchange notes on the events of the week, and to discuss strategies for the days to come.

This whole exercise not only returned the focus to Delhi, but also rejuvenated the whole party after the draining setback of the general elections. The keyword here is 'focus'. Focusing on the task at hand and achieving success with available resources makes a world of difference.

The Volunteers

The volunteers have always been the AAP's backbone. Right from their anti-corruption campaigning days, it was the volunteers' indefatigable passion and hard work that enabled 'David' to challenge 'Goliath' without the money or muscle power political outfits usually have. Yet the enthusiasm of the volunteers was at rock bottom after the general election debacle. They were not only disillusioned, but also disappointed because of the leadership problem. There was too much confusion at the top. They were disappointed because in the earlier assembly election Delhi voters had supported them, but they lost heavily in the general elections. The message was not clear (as people wanted AAP in Delhi but Modi at the Centre). At this time, AAP leader Kejriwal decided to contest LS elections on 400 seats. It became imperative to rejuvenate the volunteers. There were over 1 lakh volunteers involved in the entire Delhi election campaign. Fahim Khan, head of volunteer management for the AAP, said:

> There were broadly three categories of volunteers. Till the beginning of December, there were 30,000 volunteers from the city, a number which went up to 70,000 by February. Then there were 35,000–40,000 volunteers who were part of the online or calling campaign and phone calls were placed to residents across the city for donations and so on. The standing instruction to the volunteers was to behave courteously, like they were the staff of a five-star hotel.[13]

There were also 8000 volunteers who came from outside Delhi. While most of them were redirected to specific constituencies if they came to Delhi before 30 January, new arrivals after that date were asked to join the 'Buzz' campaign. 'This campaign was designed to draw as much attention as we could in the last days of the campaign. We had biker rallies, nukkad nataks, flash mobs and a music group called Play for Change. We identified 115 hotspots across the city, which included marketplaces, Metro stations and border areas,' says Khan.

The regional backgrounds of the volunteers were taken into consideration when they were allotted constituencies. For instance, volunteers from Punjab were sent to areas like Tilak Nagar and Rajouri Garden, while those from Uttar Pradesh and Bihar went to Poorvanchali seats.

The difference between the volunteers of AAP and those in other political parties was that AAP volunteers always felt like they were on a mission and contributing to a greater cause. Many of them left well-paying jobs to come to Delhi and help Arvind Kejriwal change the face of Indian politics.

The Jan Sabhas (Public Meetings)

After 15 December 2014, when it became clear that Delhi was headed for a February election, each day at least fifteen jan sabhas were held across the city. Some of the most important jan sabhas were led by Arvind Kejriwal. Kejriwal attended jan sabhas in each of the seventy constituencies and, in some places, more than one jan sabha at one constituency. Many negotiations materialized within the party, as the candidates were constantly pleading with the central leadership to organize an 'Arvind' jan sabha for them. The party took these requests very seriously. They were all meticulously planned. Ashish Talwar, a notoriously hard taskmaster, took charge.

While the district manager and candidate of each constituency was meant to organize the modalities of the jan sabha, deciding the location and organizing the advertisements, a national team would still arrive to review arrangements four days prior to the event.[14]

The Manifesto

In each jan sabha, the district supervisors and volunteers were tasked with spreading the message of the manifesto that was released on 31 January 2015. The planning of this process was exhausting the members. Preparation of a Delhi-specific manifesto had started in September 2014 by reaching out to the people. The idea was to use the volunteer base to conduct meetings so that ideas would emanate from the people of Delhi themselves. This also ensured engagement. Meetings were held between senior leaders of the party, and Kejriwal was often present. The decision was made to approach the manifesto through issues and not constituencies. 'The idea came up in meetings of the DECG (Delhi Election Campaign Group) and teams were formed on specific issues like women's security, issues of the youth, rural development, and urban infrastructure and so on. These groups went across Delhi for four months, discussing pressing issues with residents. Eventually, a programme was organized based on each issue and these became the backbone of our manifesto and 70-point action plan for Delhi.'[15][16]

AAP 2.0 to AAP 3.0

With Delhi getting ready to vote for the assembly elections in less than six months, the AAP and team Kejriwal decided to adopt a comprehensive communication strategy. The AAP

declared their seventy candidates by the first week of January
so they had enough time to campaign hard, while their main
competitor was busy celebrating the Lok Sabha election. Some
of the AAP's candidates were first-timers, and an early start
helped them become visible.

Their campaign's youthful style also helped the AAP
regain lost ground. A team of young, dynamic and extremely
dedicated volunteers worked to create a peppy theme song,
creative advertisements and innovative campaigns like flash
mobs. They constructed a strong presence on social media. On
1 February, shoppers in Connaught Place were surprised to
find hundreds of youngsters wearing the AAP's trademark cap
and walking along the Inner Circle, strumming guitars, singing
patriotic songs and asking people to vote for 'Mufflerman' (pet
name for party head Arvind Kejriwal). This style of effective
and visible campaigning was so impactful that competitors
were forced to duplicate it.

The most important aspect of AAP's campaign was
door-to-door communication. This certainly impacted the
masses. Each candidate went for at least one round in his or
her area. They organized nukkad sabhas (street plays) and
documentaries about the party, but nothing else.

Many ideas were products of informal conversations. With
limited finances, any expense had to be thought out long and
hard. For instance, instead of playing all day, ad jingles were only
on a radio channel for five hours during peak times. Hoardings
were only put up at places with a minimum footfall of 5000
people a day. The party decided to communicate a positive
message by talking about the work they did during their forty-
nine-day government and what they planned on doing after
regaining power. This strategy countered the negative agenda
of the Opposition parties.

Marketing Lessons from Political Campaigning

Theodore Levitt's expression 'look into the mirror instead of looking out of the window'[17] perfectly summarizes AAP's thinking during the run-up to the 2015 Delhi assembly elections.

Some age-old marketing philosophies are discussed here to help us understand the difference in AAP's poll tactics in terms of customer/voter orientation. Marketing orientation is one of the superior philosophies of running a business enterprise. The concept represents the foundation of high-quality marketing practices. In a broader sense, market orientation refers to organization-wide generation of market intelligence pertaining to current and future needs of customers, dissemination of intelligence within the organization and responsiveness to it.[18] It dictates that businesses must cultivate mindset, structure, processes and strategies that aim at satisfying customer needs and want better than the competition. It subordinates the enterprise to the will of the market. It establishes the instrumentality of business as a means of making the lives of target consumers better. Accordingly, a customer's articulation of what is appropriate for a business may differ from a manager's. The goal is to generate superior value for consumers as compared to the competitors.

Customer Orientation

Customer orientation demands keeping an unwavering focus on evolving customer needs and wants by developing responses to meet them effectively. Although Delhi may be the same physical place with the same inhabitants, between these two elections the reality has shifted. In terms of consumer choice, the primary consideration in the national election was between two brands: the BJP (with governance, inclusion and a strong spokesperson) and Congress (riddled with corruption and lacking leadership).

By exploiting the voters' frustration with Congress and carefully executing an election strategy based on inclusion and governance, the BJP led people to vote for them. This was a result of customers trying a new brand after they got disappointed from the existing brands. The shift of young voters' loyalty from the AAP to the BJP in the national elections (Congress lost its status as an alternative) was noted because the discourse in media (easy to spread) shifted back to saffron. BJP has been seen as a party of Hindu ideology. There were apprehensions among the voters, especially the minority communities, about the future when BJP came into power. Media had previously branded BJP as a saffron party, with hard-core Hindu-dominated ideologists.

This may have been satisfactory for hard-core BJP supporters, but it was certainly disappointing for the new, rational and discriminating younger class. This shows the necessity of keeping an unwavering focus on evolving customer needs and wants. BJP won all the seven Lok Sabha seats of Delhi in the general election of 2014. Last time when BJP won all the seven seats in Delhi was in 1999, under the premiership of A.B. Vajpayee. In the 2014 elections, voters lost their faith in AAP even after their good performance in previous assembly elections due to non-fulfilment of promises made. The reason for this debacle was the internal fight among AAP members.

Competitor Orientation

This refers to a mindset where a firm keeps its competitors (analysis of their strategies, strengths and weaknesses) in the centre of its strategy-development process and decides to beat them no matter the cost. It is an aggressive and reactionary mode of operation and often leads to firms ignoring customers. Beating the competition is not the mission of any business. Competitors should only assume significance when they interfere with a firm's ability to reach customers. Obsession with competitors is a recipe for disaster.

The BJP's strategy in Delhi was entirely competition oriented. Its campaign focused on AAP leaders in an aggressive and personal manner. Consider the BJP's use of words like 'mischief maker', 'thief', 'monkey', 'toxic', 'liar' and 'anarchist' in its campaign against Kejriwal. Similarly, its radio campaign tried to cast Kejriwal in poor light, but messages like 'fugitive' were irrelevant to the voters.[19] BJP's loss, despite winning a majority at the Centre, was a big shock for the Modi–Shah team. BJP was riding high on the winning tide and was confident of winning majority in the assembly elections as well. In earlier rallies, Modi restrained himself from direct attacks on the Opposition leaders. But in Delhi he openly criticized Kejriwal and even called him an 'anarchist'. Delhi voters had supported AAP in the previous assembly election because they wanted corruption to be uprooted by a clean government. Somehow, BJP in Delhi didn't focus on these issues and continuously targeted AAP leaders. In another instance, BJP declared Kiran Bedi as their CM candidate at the last moment. It showed clearly that they were under tremendous pressure from AAP's gaining traction.

6

DIGITAL MEDIA CAMPAIGNING

Political parties are continuously seeking new strategies for an increasingly digitized world where young voters are disinterested in or indifferent to politics. Digital media provides a way for political marketers to reach a huge bank of young voters. Without investing heavily on expensive mass-marketing, political parties can reach potential voters effectively through digital media channels with messages that specifically target these voters. However, political marketing targeted at young voters is challenging.[1]

Political parties do not adequately understand the country's youth or the new digital media. Anecdotal evidence suggests that young people use the Internet as their main source of political information, making this medium the most influential to their political choices.[2] Not only political parties have to use digital media to complement their traditional campaigning tools, but they also must consider it to be an integral part of their overall strategy. This is especially relevant in a country like India, where young people constitute the major part of the total population.

Recently, election campaigns have shown a distinct shift towards the use of digital media. This chapter illustrates some interesting new digital media strategies used by the political parties in their campaigns.

Efficient Use of IT, Social Media and Management Principles

The general election of 2014 was India's first where people connected through the Internet. In India, there was a general perception that social media users did not have much significance in the voting process. Political leaders remained in denial of social media's importance until Anna Hazare's movement became the talk of the town. The AAP won twenty-eight seats in Delhi assembly elections and the BJP fell short of forming a government. This was a wake-up call, especially for parties like the BJP and Congress: Congress for losing the election badly and BJP for underestimating the power of activism through social media.

On the contrary, AAP made efficient use of social media and the online tools available to them. The party used mass emails to seek funds; Facebook to share information, seek public opinion, mobilize volunteers; and Twitter campaigns to push their agenda. They made efficient use of audio conferencing, missed calls, mass calling and many other information technology tools.

Modi is the most technologically savvy politician till date, and the BJP pioneered the use of IT in efficient communication. Yet with the advent of social media tools and the rise of the AAP, the BJP seemed to be lagging behind in their IT and social media strategies. The outcome of the Delhi elections forced them back to their war room to restructure their campaign strategy.

Open-access Internet platforms allow one to reach the youth, build conversations and share and mobilize opinions towards electoral success.

Modi and his team not only used the social media platforms effectively, they also reached out to the masses with a variety of innovative platforms. Among other platforms, they used 3D holographic projections, 'Chai pe Charcha' via videoconferencing and audio-conferencing bridges to reach party workers effectively.

Arvind Gupta, IT cell convener for the BJP, implemented a communication technique where Modi's speeches during rallies could be heard over the phone by dialling a number. The user was charged as per the standard call rates. The co-author of this book helped Gupta file a patent application to maintain competitiveness and prevent political opponents from using the technology. Modi's speeches typically lasted 45–60 minutes, meaning individuals spent around Rs 45–60 per call. Subscribers could not only listen to live speeches, but they could also access recorded speeches of past rallies.

Pre-recorded clips of Modi talking about issues like inflation, development, corruption, etc., were also made available via this platform. More than 30 lakh people used this platform to listen to various speeches and recorded content. The ruling government sometimes imposed power cuts to stop people from listening to and viewing Modi on TV during the rallies, but this innovative solution of making pre-recorded speeches available over phone helped the BJP reach the masses despite power cuts, especially in rural areas.

Digital Media in Action: BJP

Android-Based and Facebook Apps

The BJP and its supporters developed numerous apps to bring efficiency and allow faster connectivity with today's tech-savvy youth. The apps India 272+ and Modi 4PM Fund were widely used. The IT team from the BJP's youth wing developed the Android app Click to Connect and the Facebook app Yuva Mitra to quickly enrol youngsters in the BJP via smartphones or Facebook.

GPS

A fleet of vehicles fitted with GPS drove through the remotest villages of UP and Bihar playing clips of Modi's speeches and the 'Modi Aane Vala Hai' song on 55-inch LED screens.

High-tech 'Chai pe Charcha' events and 3D rallies have been previously discussed. More than 1350 3D rallies were organized across the length and breadth of the country. Almost every BJP candidate wanted Modi to be present. With the BJP alone contesting for 428 seats, it was difficult for Modi to meet public demand. The 3D rallies helped him cover larger areas in a shorter span of time. Despite being a virtual avatar of Modi, the 3D holographic images were so real that people insisted that they had met Modi on the stage.

In another incident in Gujarat, Modi's 3D campaign really captured the imagination. Some villagers were so convinced that Modi was there in person that they barricaded the roads to keep him in their village. This not only captured the imagination of the common voter, but also mesmerized the Opposition leaders. Not happy with Modi's success, Congress

General Secretary Digvijaya Singh, infamous for his illogical comments, compared Modi to the ten-headed Ravana.

This technology actually helped Modi extend his reach and provide numerous opportunities to show his electorate in more than 1500 locations. He personally addressed 10 crore voters via this technology. Over 30,000 square metres of Musion's (the company supplying this technology) patented holographic projection foil; 200 Christie (digital technology) 20k and 14k projectors; 400 satellite dishes; 5500 metres of trusses, 1300 lights; 500 audio speakers; 200 sound mixers and power amps; and 14,000 metres of speaker and power cables were used in this entire high-tech 3D campaign of Modi. Musion trained over 200 crew members in various activities of installation and support. They travelled around India, working with the stages and installing Eyeliner™ system.[3]

Mission 272+

Media and political pundits were cynical of BJP's success and most were predicting a hung Parliament before the elections. Modi's conviction of attracting the majority of population in his favour was based on the following facts. In the 1999 general elections, BJP had won 183 seats, the highest ever, and stood second in another 111 seats. In 2004, BJP won 138 seats and came second in another 133 seats. Further, there were about 286 parliamentary seats that the BJP had won at least once between 1996 and 2004.

With an absolutely clear goal in mind, BJP formulated a 'volunteer mobilization' strategy. They mobilized volunteers, especially youth, via information technology and social media. Arvind Gupta spearheaded this gigantic project. The key features of the initiative included:

1. Identification of volunteers

   - Developed a website, www.india272.com, an Android app and a suite of Facebook apps.
   - Provided a toll-free number for missed calls and provided the number for free chat via SMS or WhatsApp. This gave them the contact details of the interested volunteers.
   - Built a database of interested volunteers. People who registered in this mission included members from all walks of life—graduates, ex-servicemen, NRIs, professionals, etc.
   - Did segmentation of the data according to interest areas, age and assembly/parliamentary constituency.

2. Tasks allocated

   - Distribute pamphlets
   - Connect to NGOs working for specially abled people
   - Collect data points, comparing performance of BJP- and Congress-ruled states
   - Create catchy slogans and poems for the campaign
   - Campaign at booth level
   - Keep an eye on online activities, especially on Facebook and Twitter, by other political parties
   - Make the lotus shine in their constituency
   - Seek commitment from voters. Ask them to send their voter ID card number to a designated number
   - Ensure voter turnout on the election day

Over 1 crore people were roped in under this initiative. About 10 lakh of them were working actively for the party to reach out to voters well before the elections until the end.

This programme was made appealing by providing incentives to volunteers, who introduced the maximum number of people from a region. They were acknowledged and sent a personalized message with Narendra Modi's stamp.

Mission 272+ volunteers not only did basic ground-level activities, but they also helped make Modi's rallies a grand success all over India. These volunteers distributed pamphlets and convinced people to listen to Modi and vote for 'change'.

NaMo Number: 'Mera Vote, Mera Network, Mere Liye, Desh Ke Liye'

Mission 272+ launched 'NaMo Number' 7800 7800 to seek support for Modi and mobilize volunteers. Through this platform, the volunteers were asked to build their own network of NaMo voters and get supporters to SMS their voter ID to this number while adding the respective volunteer's (mobilizer's) mobile number at the end. This helped them track who motivated the person to pledge their support for Modi. The users could measure their contribution via their NaMo number—votes that one is responsible for. That's how the volunteers were encouraged to create their network with mobile numbers of their peers. Volunteers were then asked to call and ensure that voters in their network went for voting on the polling day in their area. BJP's local unit extended full support to these new volunteers in terms of training and providing basic election-related information.

Mere Sapno ka Bharat

This programme was led by Smriti Irani, the then vice president of BJP, who is now the textiles department minister.

Under this programme, people, especially youngsters, were invited to capture their dreams and aspirations on camera. The participants had to record videos or take pictures with tag lines explaining the India of their dreams and post them on the India272 portal via the web or the Android app (i.e. Mere Sapno Ka Bharat). A point-based-selection criterion was used to select the best entry, and the opportunity to meet Narendra Modi was used to incentivize participants.

A theme song, 'Mere Sapno ka Bharat', sung by the famous Bollywood singer Shaan, was created to promote the event. The programme was launched on 26 January 2014, India's Republic Day. Again, the key idea of the programme was to increase outreach and engage people who were willing to speak out, sing or write.

War Room and National Digital Operations Centre

This team ensured that the BJP's campaigns and rallies were organized with military precision, including appropriate backup plans in case of a backlash. Centres similar to the ones in Delhi were set up in Lucknow, Varanasi and other key locations. The BJP's IT cell convener Arvind Gupta was instrumental in setting up these digital operations at BJP headquarters all over India.

This team included several professionals, intellectuals and young and enthusiastic engineers and management graduates from premier institutions. The team was responsible for establishing perfect synergy and coordination among the political, non-political and creative facets of the campaign. Team members were required to interface between the RSS and the state leaders and also to coordinate between the BJP headquarters and Modi's Gandhinagar office. Vijay

Chauthaiwale, a molecular biologist and vice president, discovery research, the research and development arm of Torrent Pharma in Ahmedabad, was responsible for this coordination, owing to his earlier association with RSS.[4]

Research, Analytics and Content Generation

Another member, Manoj Lawda, a UK-based mergers and acquisitions lawyer, headed Modi's research analysis and messaging team. He also helped set up similar control rooms in Lucknow and Varanasi. Lawda's duties were to ensure effective message delivery across the country, advise Modi on key issues of the day and assist in setting the agenda in coordination with Modi's team in Ahmedabad. He also worked closely on the campaign's creative aspects along with Piyush Pandey's team, the man who handled BJP's ad campaign, to narrate and amplify Modi's story.

The team usually started their day at 9.30 a.m. with a huddle meeting to set the agenda and decide the message context to proceed accordingly. All the party spokespersons needed to attend these meetings, news hour debates or at least be there through teleconferencing. They all required some standard and reliable information.

The team studied campaigns from around the world, including Barack Obama's. The messages and the slogans were customized to suit the Indian mindset. They also gave region-specific input for speeches in the rallies. For example, the team studied the problems faced by fishermen in coastal areas and infiltration in the North-east. Modi utilized their input in his speeches. A couple of youngsters were there to monitor the speeches made by Opposition leaders (Congress) to understand their critiques of Modi and the BJP. Within fifteen minutes of Congress's speeches, the team would craft points to counter their points. Modi would then use their input at the most opportune time and occasion. Modi made it clear that none of the opponents' questions should remain unanswered.

Pamphlets, Leaflets and Comparative Charts and Graphs

Another key responsibility of the National Digital Operations Centre (NDOC) team was to conduct research on factors affecting electoral outcomes, such as different aspects of governance, economy, policy issues and so on. The team produced comparative studies on the NDA government under Atal Bihari Vajpayee by analysing UPA's performance over the past ten years. The comparison was aesthetically engaging and presented using audiovisual aids to make it suitable for both party leaders and workers as well as the general public. A few samples of high-quality researched data can be found at http://www.bjp.org/core-issues. This data was picked up by Mission 272+ volunteers, the Bharatiya Janata Yuva Morcha (BJYM) control room and several other party functionaries who propagated the content on various social media sites, microblogging sites and chat services like WhatsApp.[5]

Research Support by CAG

Team CAG helped significantly in bringing valuable insights into the 2014 election and assisted the BJP in formulating a robust strategy backed by well-researched data. The CAG team included people from diverse backgrounds such as consulting, media, law, investment banking and public policy. After being educated at prestigious institutions like the IITs, the IIMs, ISB, Stanford and Cornell, this highly-skilled team of researchers contributed significantly to Modi's 2014 strategy.

CAG produced several detailed reports based on primary and secondary research methods. These reports were extremely helpful in understanding electoral dynamics, voting patterns, demographics, social and regional influences, prevailing moods of voters and several other determining factors of electoral outcome. CAG's website[6] provides a crisp description of each of these reports; these have been included nearly verbatim below.

1. Constituency-wise reports: Parliamentary constituency, assembly constituency, village ward and booth-level analysis. This data was used to prepare a strategy for around 6 lakh polling booths in twelve states. This activity was used to optimize resource allocation.

2. Retrospective analysis: Using the electoral data of the last six elections to segment booths across 400 parliamentary constituencies. This data of previous elections was then used to analyse the trend of voting in previous elections. Later on, it was aligned with the exit poll results to gauge the sentiment of voters. CAG gave these reports to Modi's core team. Demographic and socio-economic information was also used during segmentation of the polling booths and constituencies. CAG prepared structured documents like presentations for all the constituencies. CAG representatives used an extensive research to prepare these documents which were given to BJP's think tank. These were the typical insights or research reports with information like voter population, gender ratio, education level and previous election data of that particular constituency. The report also shows parameters of analysis

like win-to-loss record, margin, vote share average and polling percentage. CAG used census data of 2011 and 2001 to create the demographic profile of a constituency.

3. Real-time opinion poll analysis: Data collection from personal interviews carried out by CAG volunteers on the field as a real-time event. The data collected from these interviews was sent back to the analytics room, where analysts generated trends and findings. The results were then forwarded to field units to minimize turnaround time. This saved effort and increased the time to re-strategize.

4. In-depth social listening exercise: Key members or opinion leaders were brought to discuss topical scenarios like India's social and political condition. These interviews explained local electoral patterns and preferences. Interviews were analyzed and reports were sent to the core team. These interviews were done on a daily basis, with the report reaching the campaign management support team at the end of each day.

5. Rapid action report: A combination of past trends, current opinion polls and social view were collected to prepare a rapid action report, or a snapshot of the evolving picture of the constituency that resembled the reality on ground. This enabled the decision makers to get the right picture in advance and saved time in coming up with new strategies. Also, information generated by rapid action reports was concrete because it was not completely based on opinion polls.

6. Sentiment analysis: Information from the news, social media and grapevine channels was extracted by modern-day tools like language-processing software and texting patterns. This information was then used to calculate the extent and polarity (positive/negative) of the popular

sentiment for a given entity (say Narendra Modi). The outputs were used to fine-tune the quality and capacity of the social media campaign.

7. Social media analytics: Demographic and geographic profiling of Internet users done through analysis of metrics such as the number of user interactions, the theme of posts, etc.

8. CAG presence prioritization model: This was based on social, political and economic factors. Based on analysis in more than 400 cities across the country, team CAG prepared a prioritization order. Based on this information, CAG prolonged its activities and opened chapters in twenty-nine cities across India.

9. Mega charge sheet: This fifty-six-page document contained a charge sheet for the Central government and every non-NDA state and an achievement sheet for every NDA state in the country—from Kerala to Kashmir.

Digital Media in Action: AAP

AAP initiated Delhi Dialogue in 2014 to increase people's collaboration in policymaking. This was an open platform meant to engage domain experts from various fields and build realistic plans in twelve different areas of focus with the goal of making Delhi a world-class city by 2020. This effectively engaged common citizens of Delhi, getting them to share their concerns on various issues related to jobs and employment, women's rights and safety, social welfare and social justice, energy and electricity, health, rural Delhi, trade and industry, sanitation and solid-waste management, transportation, education, land and housing, and water. Citizens could give their suggestions on different policy areas through AAP's website, text messaging or registering for round-table meetings.

The initiative was primarily aimed to challenge the age-old practices of releasing manifestos before polling, which, according to AAP leaders, was a way to escape discussion. Instead of telling people what the party could do for them, AAP volunteers had discussions with voters to understand their desires and hopes. The best points raised during these discussions were added to the party's manifesto.

At the launch, AAP's President Arvind Kejriwal said:

> We wish to know what the expectations of the people are and how they want their Delhi to be. We will interact with professionals, housewives, students, youth, women, people from villages, industrialists, people from JJ cluster and unauthorized colonies. We will then prepare a 50-point programme, prepare a blue-print and address these issues.[7]

Paanch Saal Kejriwal (Five Years of Kejriwal)

The AAP adopted a concrete strategy for the Delhi assembly elections and it paid off. Similar communication strategy had been adopted by BJP for the 2014 general election and by Barack Obama in the 2008 US presidential elections. It is important to mention that any concrete communication strategy requires key agenda points, which are feasible and must be delivered. Subsequently, it has to have direct connection with people (in this case, voters). In their election campaign, the AAP tried to communicate issues that were relevant and prominent.

Let us look at some of the important communications proposed by AAP while campaigning.

Concrete Agenda	Communication
Delhi Jan Lokpal	Bring more power to investigate and prosecute against corruption
Swaraj Bill	'Power to People', decision-making power to local community people
Full statehood for Delhi	Giving Delhi more power, Delhi Police, DDA, MCD and other bodies
Electricity bills to be cut by half	CAG audit for electricity companies
DISCOM portability	Right to consumers to select their service provider
Solar city	Shift to renewable and alternate sources of energy
Right to 'water'	Universal access to drinking water at an affordable price, as a 'citizen's right'
Free water	Free water up to 20 kilolitres per month
Reviving 'Yamuna'	Cleaning of the Yamuna, the lifeline of Delhi, through extensive sewer network and sewage-treatment plans.
Public toilets/loos	1.5 lakh toilets in slums across the city, 50,000 toilets in public spaces, 1 lakh toilets for women
New schools	500 new schools to ensure easy access to quality education
New colleges	Twenty new colleges under Delhi administration in partnership with nearby villages
Regulate 'fees'	Regulation of private school fees, online structure and accountants

(Contd.)

Concrete Agenda	Communication
E-Governance	All government forms and services to be made available online, extensive data collection on government projects; progress will be posted online
'Smart Delhi'	Free Wi-Fi, 10,000 CCTV cameras in DTC buses and crowded places

Source: 'Delhi elections 2015: How a small IIT-B team shaped AAP's Delhi poll campaign', *Times of India*, 12 February 2015.

Digital Media in Action: US Presidential Campaigns

When we talk about communication, we look at the delivery side and content. It was Barack Obama's new media communication strategy and his promise for change that caused young people to prefer his party[8]. This strategy contributed to the election results. This mechanism was made to promote Obama by building communities and enabling and promoting bottom activities. By the time the campaign started, these ideas were blooming. Social networks like Facebook and Twitter and user-generated sites like YouTube and Wikipedia were the main modes of modern media communication. The media strategy of his opponents was ineffective and failed to harness the power of communities and user activities.

Poll results[9] show the power of Obama's communication strategy: his supporters were armed with concrete messages from his campaign, like 'change', 'hope' and 'unity'. This had strong dissemination value. The poll was conducted by the Harvard Institute of Politics (IOP) in April 2008. The fact

that respondents chose 'character' over 'experience' suggests
that Obama became an individual to his supporters not just a
distant politician.

The underlying idea of Obama's campaign strategy
was community organization. It was Obama's initiative
to build his campaign from the bottom-up and apply his
community-organizing experience to politics. Obama
inspired a nationwide constituency by narrating his own
story to Democrats. His story of hope, American culture
and its strength as a community, and his skill of public
narrative, energized the audience of US. Obama talked
about 'action' required to achieve those values. His skills as a
gifted orator helped him to connect directly with the voters.
He talked about 'hope' for young Americans and 'moral
reforms' in the best American tradition. By 2007, it was
pretty clear that Obama was going to adopt the organizing
strategy that incorporated new media tools. As noted by
Ganz[10], 'Value based organizing invites people to skip "issue
silos" and unite as human beings'. A key distinction between
organizing and mobilizing is one-to-one meetings held to
initiate a working relationship. It is above the simple pledge
of support or donation or signature campaign. Obama's
campaign attracted young organizers from New Hampshire
Dean campaign in 2004.

The campaign strategy was designed in such a way that
it enabled people to use their powers—volunteering, creating
online videos, blogging, etc. Campaign strategists were
successful in making people believe that they belonged to and
were supported by the Obama camp, so the campaign itself
became a big community.

It is important to mention that this was the most
expensive presidential campaign in the US history. During

the 2008 campaign, Obama raised and spent more money than any other candidate ever has. According to data from the Center for Responsive Politics website, OpenSecrets.org, in 2004 Bush and Kerry spent around $300 million each on campaigning. In 2008, McCain spent almost $400 million and Obama spent $800 million, almost twice the amount of McCain.[11]

Obama invested almost three times more money into media than his competitor. Obama's spending on broadcast media was about four times that of McCain's and on Internet campaigning almost five times. Various researchers in their work on political campaigning concluded that his media strategy was far more conceptually advanced than McCain's.

Mediatization

'Mediatization' is a common political buzzword. It has impacted every sphere of society in its ever growing coverage, be it in terms of globalization, economic reform, financial crisis or political change. The media has played a major role in strengthening the democratic voice of the nation.[12]

Defining Mediatization and Media Logic

Mediatization is a contextual term in communication research. It can be defined through media, which comprises the infiltration, expansion and fusion of culture with different sub areas, of which political systems are also considered a vital part. It can be argued that the media is growing as an institution in its autonomous capacity. This drives politicians and political parties to construct their communication strategy according to the way the media functions. The influence

of mass media on various aspects of political system puts a
great focus on the changes it has brought along in its new
role in politics. Firstly, Kent Asp, a Swedish media researcher,
spoke about the mediatization of political life, or the process
whereby 'a political system to a high degree is influenced
by and adjusted to the demands of the mass media in their
coverage of politics.'[13]

The evolution of the US presidential elections shows the
growing presence of these concepts. It must be noted that
the reach of the media doesn't stop at influencing politics;
it goes as far as even influencing political communication.
These are tailor-made communications, media-oriented and
clubbed together in media's own news coverage. It leads to
metacoverage, which is a logical consequence of mediatization.
According to Nika Stracabosko, while mediatization covers
the politics oriented around the media, metacoverage refers
to coverage of the reactions of the politicians. This was done
by taking communication specifically tailored to be media-
orientated, content in the news media, as well as publicity
efforts of candidates, and then combining all of these factors in
the media's own news coverage. So the term 'metacoverage' can
be explained as (a) coverage of the behaviours, products and
performance of the news media and (b) coverage of candidates'
use of paid media, communication personnel, and other forms
of strategic communication.[14]

It is a reactionary process, influencing the public discourse
that is transmitted by the media. It is a kind of defensive
reaction by journalists who are attempting to regain control
over content. Journalists were once passive communicators
who disseminated information about political figures. This
new strategy of mediatization has helped them evolve from
the background to speak about themselves, making comments,

sharing their experiences and even showing their skills at covering the news.[15]

According to the mediatization theory of Krotz[16], media is a modification of face-to-face communication or a technical institution through which people communicate; it also has impact on culture and societies. As the communication environment is becoming complicated, it brings social and cultural changes. Therefore it can take various forms and shapes. It denotes a descriptive concept that allows scholars to trace processes of institutional adaption to the media.[17] As Krotz puts it, mediatization is necessary if we want to conceptualize and empirically analyse dramatic changes in media and communication. The concept of mediatization should therefore be committed to empirical analysis to help study the process among the population.[18]

Unlike Donges[19], Strömbäck[20] did not limit his study to one level of analysis but argued that mediatization is multidimensional in nature and is a highly process-orientated concept that can be divided into four phases, which are neither linear nor unidirectional but highly correlated. The first phase is achieved with the reach of media into the most important source of information and channel of communication.

The second phase involves the media becoming more independent of governmental or political bodies. In the third phase, it increases its independence and importance. The fourth phase is when the social and political players internalize the media's logic in their governing system. Strömbäck pointed out that these four phases are somewhat idealized, but they all offer a means of thinking about the process of mediatization that allows comparisons across different times and countries.

Media logic refers to the rules of the media, which are defined by selection, organization, presentation and information recognition.[21] It can be understood as a way of interpreting and covering social, cultural and political phenomena.[22] Altheide and Snow[23] defined it as a form of communication through which media presents and transmits information. Media logic's primary goal is to receive media attention. Election campaigns become the obvious choice of media attention due to media representation. This could be attributed to the decline in public broadcasting, emergence of commercial television with its multitude of channels that run through the day and night. The advent of the Internet has resulted in the segregation of audiences.

Researchers, through their constant efforts, understood the changes in society and media by developing new forms of political communication. US presidential elections could be seen as a system of communication campaigning. US elections are characterized by fundraising campaigns, which get considerable coverage in the media. Earlier campaigns were dominated by newspaper and radio messages where volunteers worked at grass-roots level. In the 1990s, campaigns were transformed by the presence of television, news and marketing strategies. This confirms the notion that campaigns must use the media to convey a candidate's information and their position on issues.

India, like many other countries in the world, has a multiparty system where political parties use various means of communication to attract voters. In contrast, the United States of America has only two major political parties that have been contesting each other for over 200 years. Both parties make use of new media, new techniques, new electronic gadgets and new research methods to garner attention; the

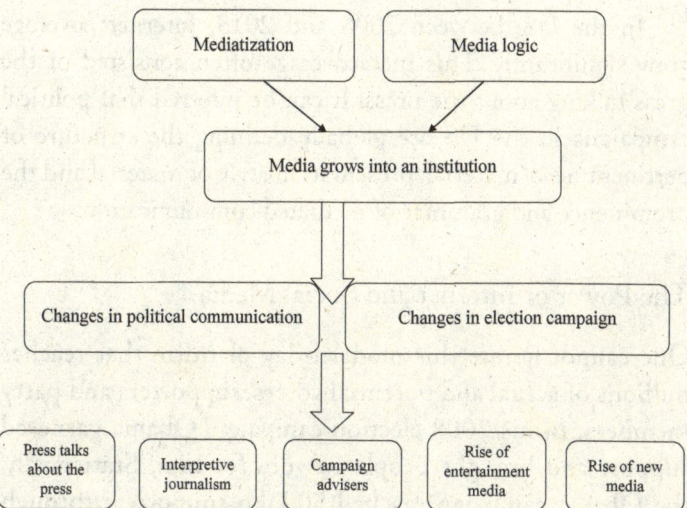

Figure: The effect of mediatization and media logic on election campaigns.

level of innovation used in making campaigns attractive is commendable.

According to a book written by Plasser and Plasser,[24] political campaigns across the world are becoming increasingly similar to the US presidential election campaigns. They studied the political aspects of many countries such as Australia, New Zealand, Ukraine, Russia, Georgia, Belarus and India, as well as many African and East Asian countries. They found that in each country the use of electronic media, social media and research methods varied greatly. They also found that most of the countries felt that American campaigns could be easily transferred to their countries. It was emphasized that fundraising and image-building campaigns of the US were admired and replicated successfully in many countries.

In the US, between 2008 and 2013, Internet coverage grew significantly. This metacoverage often consisted of the press talking about the press. It can be inferred that political campaigns in the US are globally defining the structure of pertinent news material, presentation style of material and the prominence and grammar of mediated communication.

The Power of Internet and Social Media

One cannot ignore this modern-day platform that reaches millions of actual and potential voters, supporters and party members. In his 2008 election campaign, Obama garnered support and brought people to vote for him. Statistically, the Obama campaign reached 50 lakh supporters through fifteen different social networks. In the duration of his campaign, he harnessed 25 lakh Facebook supporters, 1.15 lakh Twitter followers and 5 crore viewers for his YouTube channels.[25]

A few communication lessons can be drawn specifically from a strategic point of view:

1. Prompt and early advertising of intent: It is very important to start communicating with supporters and voters as early as possible. In the Delhi assembly elections of 2014, the AAP took the centre stage quite early. They made all possible communication with voters who had trusted them in the last elections. They struck the initial chords while the BJP, their main opposition, was busy celebrating their victory in the general election.
2. Advanced booking of advertisements in media: In the 2012 election, Obama spent less money on average buying and placing ads than his competitor Mitt Romney.

3. Data analytics: There is no need to play on intuitions when data analytics is available. In US elections, data analysers play a vital role in providing 'experiment-driven and information-oriented' programmes. This is not approximation work but actual tracking of voter behaviour.

4. Mobiles and their users: Smartphones have made it quite simple for both the sender and the receiver to stay connected. This gives instant access to information that one wants to disseminate to one's voters or supporters.

5. Microblogging websites: Twitter can be a platform for dialogue with minimal words to express positively or negatively.

6. Control of in-house communication: Bringing in experts in the domains of mobile communication, data mining, coding and web development can be helpful. The kind of volume generated through these media needs to have skilled workforce.

In 2009, the Ford Motor Company developed and implemented an innovative social media and viral marketing campaign for the US launch of the Ford Fiesta subcompact car. The campaign was named the 'Ford Fiesta Movement'.

The most important part of the campaign was that the marketers of Ford had clear objectives and defined their evaluation metrics in advance. Ford let the seed consumers (agents) use the car in the hope that they would share their experiences using online social media platforms so that others could vicariously experience the car. The agents were asked to create and disseminate user-generated content such as photos, videos, blog posts, tweets and Facebook updates.

Some objectives when using social media as a communication tool are:

1. Understanding the viral marketing campaigns, and how online social media platforms can be used to distribute messages. This functions as a tool to serve brand-related content.
2. Where do the viral marketing campaigns fit in the overall marketing activity?
3. The targeting of the customers (voters) through viral social media campaigns.

Social media has played a crucial role not only in new product launches, but also in times of crisis. On 11 July 2011, more than 9,00,000 customers in Northern Illinois were left without power after a massive storm hit the area. It was hot and humid summer season. Commonwealth Edison (ComEd) crew and reinforcements from more than a dozen other states worked for days afterwards to restore the services. Simultaneously, ComEd's customer operations division worked around the clock to respond to posts from customers on the social networking sites Facebook and Twitter. This communication during a crisis, and when ComEd was being criticized for its plan to raise electricity rates, strengthened relationships with customers and the general public. This is consistent with an important corporate goal: 'Keep the lights on and information flowing.'

In the case of a natural disaster like this one, there is not much an organization can do. ComEd officials, despite knowing that this was not their fault, immediately took to Facebook and Twitter and tried to provide vital information to customers. This approach of using social media was a proactive strategy as opposed to a traditional one. Social media provided a direct platform to ComEd officials to interact with the people. This was used to answer questions about the extent of the damage and the progress of restoration efforts.

Twitter

Modi is one of the earliest politicians to use the microblogging site Twitter. By July 2014, he had become the fourth most followed world leader.[26]

Modi remains connected with his followers via Twitter, often sharing information about his governance and policy decisions. He maintains relations with prominent leaders by conveying birthday wishes to global political leaders, congratulatory notes on national days and any important event pertaining to a country. He promptly took notice of Sonia Gandhi's illness and wished her well. Modi tweeted on Sonia Gandhi's discharge from the hospital, 'Glad to know that Sonia ji's health is fine. Wishing her the best of health in future.'[27] He promptly reacts to events of national or international importance, from Nepal's earthquake to wishing players luck in sports.

He has frequently used Twitter to bait opponents. On the issue of policy paralysis, Sonia Gandhi, Manmohan Singh and other UPA ministers have faced severe criticism from Modi.

During his election campaigns, he shared pictures, videos and other information from his campaign trail. There is also an unofficial Twitter army that retaliates to negative tweets about Modi. There have been several instances of 'tweet wars' where Congress or AAP workers have tried to launch attacks against Modi or the BJP. Volunteers were quick to counter these attacks with factual information.

Similarly, Twitter handles for the BJP and its sister organizations have amassed huge followings. The BJP has over 14 lakh followers on Twitter. Several other BJP leaders have massive followings on Twitter—for example, Sushma Swaraj has over 20 lakh followers. The massive follower base of the BJP and its leadership was widely exploited to communicate key messages to voters before and during elections.

Facebook Profiles

Modi joined Facebook in 2009. His page had 80 lakh fans by December 2013 and by 6 March 2014, when the elections were announced, the number had reached 1.1 crore. By the last lap of elections, on 12 May 2014, Modi had gained 28.7 per cent more fans. He had crossed 1.4 crore fans and had become the second most 'liked' politician after Obama. As of March 2015, Modi had about 2.8 crore Facebook fans, while Obama had over 4.5 crore fans.

On 13 April 2014, Modi posted a picture of his meeting with Rajinikanth, a Tamil actor with a larger-than-life persona. This photo showed Modi being greeted by the actor. This picture was liked by 15 lakh Facebook users, shared by more than 86,000 and commented upon by more than 36,000 followers. This is an example of how effective and quick this medium has proven to be for reaching audiences free of charge.

Other Facebook Pages

Because of individual leaders running their pages, a large number of users have been connected via the official page of the BJP, the BJYM and several other sister organizations and cells of the party. Before the election's commencement, the BJP had about 24 lakh followers. By 1 January 2014, they had more than 71 lakh. Similarly, the BJYM page had 5000 followers in July 2013, but by the time of the general election they had gathered over 10 lakh followers. The BJYM's central IT team, which the co-author of this book was a member of, played a pivotal role in running a perpetual campaign that brought over 10 lakh followers to the page.

These official pages acted as key communication platforms during the entire election campaign, mobilizing volunteers, supporters and voters. Party policy positions, press conference details, poster designs, banners, advertisements, vote appeals, details of the voter registration process and several other pieces of information were shared on these pages.

Video Calls/Google Hangout

Modi not only used Facebook and Twitter effectively and wisely, but he was also the first Indian politician to connect with the youth using Google Hangout. Later, Google Hangout became more popular among youth as well as other politicians. In September 2013, he spent two hours video-broadcasting on Google+ and was viewed by 82,000 people live on YouTube from 116 countries. Modi now has more than 3 lakh people in his G+ circle. Within a week of its recording, this session was viewed by nearly 5,55,000 people. This is comparable to the 7,12,000 views that US President Barack Obama's Hangout session got in nine months.

During election season, many top BJP leaders did numerous Hangout sessions to connect with different sections of the society. Then leader of the Opposition Arun Jaitley,

BJP General Secretary P. Muralidhar Rao, BJP spokesperson Meenakshi Lekhi, BJP Vice President Smriti Irani and several others conducted Hangout sessions to connect with potential voters and answer their queries.

Websites

BJP's official website (www.bjp.org) was used as a source for official content on policy matters as well as material for campaigns such as videos, poster designs, pamphlets, etc. Another extensively used platform was that of Mission 272+. A dedicated website (www.india272.com) was created for this purpose.

Using his official website, Modi effectively delivered information and engaged with his audience. He frequently wrote on his blog and posted on this website.

Modi for PM Fund and One Vote One Note Programme

The Modi for PM Fund was launched on 14 January 2014 to secure financial support from the general public and from BJP supporters and sympathizers.

A dedicated web page (www.donate.bjp.org) was designed for online donations. Offline, volunteers of the party were given mobile-enabled donation options, wherein people could donate through mobile payment gateways and SMSs. All donors received an SMS as soon as their payment was made, which was followed by a paper receipt. When the above two modes of payment were not possible, a hundi (plastic pot) was designed and given to local party functionaries to reach out and seek support.

BJP's target was to reach 10 crore households and seek one note for each vote. The BJP's think tank believed that if a family extended financial support, it was likely that they would also vote for the party in the elections. Thousands of party workers and volunteers across India were engaged in running this campaign.

YouTube

Modi and the BJP thoroughly utilized the power of the Internet. Modi has a YouTube channel, where his team uploads all relevant video content including rallies, interviews, documentaries and much more. Modi's YouTube channel has over 2,15,000 subscribers.

Internet TV Channel: Yuva TV

Yuva TV is BJP's own Internet TV Channel. At the time of writing this book, it had over 74,000 subscribers on YouTube. The channel provided customized video solutions during the elections. It produced small video clips containing powerful messages, created documentaries to educate voters, sought public opinions, etc. It also tracked all key BJP activities, such as press conferences, programmes, events, parliamentary speeches by leaders and other forms of useful video content.

Audio Conferencing

The BJP used this platform to communicate with thousands of party workers across India. Modi and other various senior party leaders and organizational secretaries all used this platform. Senior party leaders, generally hesitant to use technology, became enthusiastic after they realized the benefits of this technology. Party organizational secretary Ramlal once mentioned that it became easy for a person like him to convey messages to and seek feedback from thousands of party workers and office-bearers over the phone while sitting at the party headquarters. It not only made the communication fast, but also saved the burden and cost of unnecessary travel. Using this platform, over 5000 people can be connected at a time.

Modi utilized this platform to reach out to more than 10,000 workers through a fifteen-minute phone call. He talked to volunteers, first-time voters and other members who had registered with various BJP platforms created for this purpose. Getting a direct call from Modi was like a dream come true for these young and enthusiastic volunteers.

He interacted with over 2000 Mission 272+ volunteers on 20 February 2014. He usually talked to them between 7.30 p.m. and 8 p.m. In this interactions, he focused on ground activities, the Vote for India campaign and advised them to use social media with caution. He also used it to spread awareness on the issue of EPIC number (Electors' Photo Identity Card number).

Calling Bihar Party Office-Bearers and Workers

Part of Modi's agenda was to focus on the two Hindu heartland states of Uttar Pradesh and Bihar. This was a first-of-its-kind high-tech exercise through which Modi addressed 1500 BJP workers from the state, including those from the panchayat level. It came a few days after Nitish Kumar, CM of Bihar, cut his seventeen-year-old ties with the BJP over Modi's elevation.

Data Collection via Missed Calls, WhatsApp and SMS

A dedicated toll-free number that allowed people to pledge support through missed calls was made available via the India 272+ platform. This number could also be used to send one's mobile number via a WhatsApp message. Another number was provided for people to pledge to support Modi via an SMS. If BJP sources are to be believed, over 13 crore people were reached via these platforms.

SMS, WhatsApp Messaging, Missed Calls and Email Campaign

As discussed under Mission 272+,[28] the BJP used IT and social media platforms extensively to garner massive support and mobilize volunteers for its mission. For example, BJP's youth wing, headed by Anurag Thakur, ran an extensive email campaign that was managed and overseen by the co-author of this book. The 'Yuva Mitra—Yuva Sadashya Abhiyan' membership drive was put in place to register new members for the youth wing. During this programme, its Facebook page (BJYM4INDIA) and Twitter page (@BJYM) were also promoted. The programme attracted over 5 lakh subscribers between July 2013 and December 2013. Today the BJYM's Facebook page has over 10 lakh followers.

Music Campaigns and Support: Songs, Caller Tunes and Ringback Tones

The BJP engaged professional artistes and musically enthusiastic volunteers to come up with catchy caller tunes and ringback tones. 'Modi Aane Vala Hai', a song sung by noted

Bollywood singer Udit Narayan, was the most popular caller tune on mobile phones and most played over the Internet. Modi's caller tunes were downloaded by over 1,00,000 people[29] and viewed on YouTube by several hundreds and thousands on official and unofficial channels.

There were many individuals and groups that wrote songs, poems and lyrics in support of Modi.

Recently, assembly elections in Delhi witnessed terrific use of digital media and social media. It is important to understand that merely creating a fan page or user accounts on different popular social media platforms is not going to fetch any positive results. One must utilize social media in a determined manner to influence the maximum number of people. BJP's general election campaign and its leader Modi used these platforms very decisively. A similar trend was followed by the AAP in the 2015 Delhi assembly elections.

Just two months before the Delhi election, a team of IIT engineers was hired to create a social media strategy. These students developed an algorithm that monitored more than a thousand tweets and messages on social media, paying special attention to their language, and analysed voters' sentiments and reactions to various issues that concerned the AAP, the state and its leaders. The results and analysis were conveyed to the AAP leadership in Delhi who used this data to fine-tune the party's election strategy and their interactions with voters. This algorithm was also used to gauge the swing in Delhi voters' mood.

One of the team members from IIT, Divyank Agarwal, said:

Corruption is an important issue that affects all of us today, particularly the 'Aam Aadmi'. Most political parties and leaders in India talk about development, good roads, improved technology etc. Arvind Kejriwal is among the handful of leaders in India who raised the issue of corruption throughout his campaigning.[30]

These engineers started their work with visits to party offices in Mumbai and devised a tool to connect with voters through social media. No doubt, they made a spectacular debut in elections, riding on strong support from the labour and lower-class section of NCT or NCR. The party had a strong presence on social networking websites such as Facebook, Twitter and YouTube. With 5.37 lakh followers on Twitter and 16 lakh fans on Facebook, the Aam Aadmi Party has leveraged benefits of social media as a means of advertising its transparent image and a simple way of voicing opinions. Many young online users were persuaded to bolster AAP ideology using social media. They had evolved from a small group, fighting against corruption, to a large-level movement. Its offline agendas and philosophies are clearly reflected on Facebook and Twitter.

According to the MTS (Mobile Tele Systems) election tracker, the AAP trended at almost the same level as the BJP with their 40,079 subscribers.[31] The political journey of the party was shared on YouTube and on other social networking platforms, showing their consistency with message delivery.

Content Strategy and Engagement

Corruption-free Delhi, the main agenda for the Aam Aadmi Party, allowed them to emerge as one of the most effective and influential political parties. The consistency of their message and its delivery in their media campaign, especially on digital media, played an important part in their popularization.

The AAP's agenda was to:

1. Catch voters' authentic opinions and increase penetration.
2. Spread awareness about party movements.
3. Unify their agenda, keeping online and offline messages in sync.
4. Connect with youth. Influence and bring them in.

They were successful in delivering the message that they were small, outnumbered and relatively new in political domain. They created ads that appealed to people emotionally using motivational images and strong content. The AAP used Twitter more effectively than they used Facebook. For a political party, this makes absolute sense because Twitter has a more mature audience.[32]

As per the Twitter India information, though during the election period Modi was the most popular leader on Twitter, AAP and Arvind Kejriwal did well and remained at the second position. Right from the days of the Jan Lokpal movement and later as an AAP leader, Kejriwal was very active on Twitter. His 'anti-establishment' image was an instant hit with the young and working-class voters who participated in the Delhi Jan Lokpal movement. His entry into politics could not be timelier as Congress had no good, politically correct orator and Modi was the only eloquent firebrand. According to Roy Chowdhury, 'He is the proverbial Pied Piper, who leads the media to set his own agenda like a band-master with shrill decibel rhetoric.'[33] In fact, Kejriwal successfully countered all the attacks made by the Opposition leaders on social media. His Internet meme (on Twitter and Facebook) became a talking point among the meme generators. At the time of election, Arvind Kejriwal's Twitter handle had 70 lakh followers. His tweets were among the most retweeted during the election time. He was trolling his opponents regularly.

Their strategy of using hashtags on Twitter worked brilliantly. A hashtag is used by people to search for a common topic. A hashtag placed before a tweet categorizes it, making it easier to find. Hashtags are commonly used for large group activities and in online conventions. The AAP trended heavily when they used #KejriwalAtKanpur, keeping their fans from across the country updated on their every move.

Utilization of Social Media Effectively

The political party had a similar strategy on Facebook. With a large number of fans listed as members, the AAP party regularly posted videos of their rallies, street plays and other campaign activities on Facebook.

The content of the AAP's message was same both online and offline, making their communications seamless. The public related to the AAP's objectives and they were made to believe that if they supported AAP, they would be party members not outsiders. This message was first communicated on a website by requesting donations for a larger cause. The party was very particular about their donation strategy. In India, political donation is normally sourced through industrialists, business houses, close aids and a good number of deposits come from the parallel economy, i.e. black money. The AAP was eager to bring in clean money through online donations and shared all possible information about donations on their website.

Videos

Videos are useful tools for connecting with people if their content is interesting. The AAP developed different types of videos—for example, one showed party chief Arvind Kejriwal telling people how they could join the party. The message was simple and clear, without any ambiguity. It delivered a strong message to voters that 'we are simple and helpful'. It served the basic objective of the campaign—to spread awareness. Statistically, AAP video ratings have been much higher than those of the BJP and Congress.[34]

Print Media Mentions

Leading print media outlets, such as *Business Standard*, the *Economic Times* and the *Times of India*, keenly followed the activities of the AAP throughout the campaign, though most of the print media focused on their negative aspects.

According to Rahul Jain, director of digital marketing and sales, Social Rajneeti, a digital marketing solution provider:[35]

> Aam Aadmi Party has been active in shaping revolutionary Indian politics since 2014 and has taken a major position among national parties in the 2014 general election. On social media, the party covered every aspect of the elections, from communicating details about political campaigns, discussing agendas, volunteering opportunities, membership drives and other content to uploading effective and thought provoking videos and closely connecting with their audience through Google Hangouts.[36]

It is an undeniable fact that social media played an important role in the AAP's victory in the Delhi elections, and it has the capacity to replicate similar results in the general elections. Besides reinforcing the fact that AAP has been doing everything it promised to do, they are also using social media to brilliantly display their daily activities.[37]

US Presidential Election 2008

Online Activities

Howard Dean was the first person to validate the power of online communities as a new media strategy for election campaigns. He said that one has to build a community, not just to enable fund raising. One needs to listen and be willing to lead.[38] Dean's campaign, which centred on listening to supporters' ideas, evolved into a movement that was run by supporters and driven by communities. MeetUp.com was a newborn start-up at that time, and it became a tool to help regular citizens plan local gatherings for their communities.

The Internet first revealed its fundraising potential in 2000 in the US. Over the next two or three years, it became clear that money could be raised effectively online. The online population's response to fundraising notices was uncertain.

Building Web Content:

barackobama.com

This website is another example of the bottom-up initiative that played a crucial role in the development of online political communication.

Volunteers inspired people to generate content about Obama and he used this content effectively. By encouraging people to participate in campaigning and by giving them ideas about the various ways in which they could contribute or promote content, Obama overtook other candidates.

Online Advertising

Right from the beginning of his campaign, Obama spent $300 million on online ads and gave 70 per cent of this money to Google. This means Obama almost outspent Clinton on Google by a 10:1 ratio. Obama's digital marketing efforts included search and display advertisements that were viewed as consistent in their messages and integrated well with his offline campaign.

As quoted by Business Insider, Obama spent more on online ads than what it cost to build the Lincoln Memorial.[39]

In the 2012 US presidential elections, when Barack Obama was running for re-election, he spent record amounts of money on online advertising, spending more than twice as much as his Republican rivals. His campaign activity spent the most on Comcast.net, paying more than $1 million for ads that have appeared on the website more than 23.8 crore times. These ads were also used as pop-ups on news websites such as CNN and the *New York Times*. These ads were also posted on some unusual places such as—Games.com, eLyrics.net and Match.com.[40]

Moat.com, an ad search engine that provides search tools for brands to find where these ads are running, featured Obama's images in 145 online ads. The ads featured Obama and his wife, sometimes along with their daughters, in family pictures. There was even one ad that features their dog, Bo.

The messages encouraged people to 'Enter to win dinner with Barack' or 'Wish Michelle a Happy Mother's Day' by clicking the ad.[41]

Organizing for Action (OFA)

A fundamental change in the online world occurred after the 2004 election with the steep rise of online communities. 'OFA is a movement of millions of Americans, coming together to fight for real, lasting change.'[42]

> With more than 250 local chapters around the country, OFA volunteers are building this organization from the ground up, community by community, one conversation at a time. Organizing for Action is a movement of millions of Americans, coming together to fight for real, lasting change.[43]

Extensive Flooding on Web Platforms

Team Obama understood it well that the 2008 election would be 'Internet election', and the next President-Elect would become a 'highly considered purchase' (a marketing term) for online users. Team research on Internet searchers claimed that success in attracting voters would depend on a strong online presence.

The aim of all candidates was to get into search results for news, images, videos and blogs.

Extensive Use of Free Platforms

Obama was well represented on all the widespread and well-known social networking and content-sharing sites as well as the less-trafficked ones. He had accounts on all major sites, including MySpace, MeetUp.com, Twitter, Flickr and Facebook, and also on some of the more professional networks, such as LinkedIn, Digg, Eventful, BlackPlanet, Eons, AsianAve, MiGente, FaithBase, Glee, Batanga and DNC party builder.

Data shows that Obama was far more active than other candidates in updating his profiles.

Mobile Texting

The *New York Times* called it, 'the biggest text messaging experiment ever'.[44] By the end of the election campaign, Team Obama had 1 crore cell numbers in their database, the majority of which belonged to young people aged 18–27.

As with every new media tool that was involved in the campaign, the campaign's mobile strategy was based on people's habits. In other words, Obama's crew knew why and how voters used their cell phones, and they provided users with all possible ways of using their phones to connect with the candidate. Young people use cell phones not only for texting and talking, but also for playing games and accessing the Internet. The Obama campaign did not limit itself to phone banking and texting; they also made Obama ringtones and wallpapers. There was even an iPhone application, Obama08, which allowed people to share their address books with the campaign and its volunteers. Once the database began to grow, Team Obama started using it not only for communicating with users, but also for mobilizing them for local events. Obama's campaign was the only presidential campaign that regionalized its base, which was important for organizing people during rallies and providing them with the local information they needed.

Online Videos: YouTube Channel

Obama's YouTube channel became one of the most popular YouTube channels. It looked like a TV network because they had no limitations on time, money or technical standards. It was not popular just because it was on the Internet, or because of the popularity of the candidate, but also because of the quality of the channel itself. His channel combined the standards of a professional network with the benefits of online television. The online videos were 'carefully designed videos' in different genres (interviews, stories and music videos). The *New York Times* magazine referred to Obama's online content as a steady diet for YouTubers.[45] The channel showed the latest content from the campaign and focused on the community rather than only on Obama. The team uploaded 1800 videos during the campaign, ranging in length from fifteen seconds to forty minutes. Their videos were viewed over 11 crore times in total.[46]

Social Media in Action: Putin in Russia

To make his claims seem viable to world leaders, Vladimir Putin used secretive social media propagandists to highlight the Ukraine issue. It is commonly accepted that all social media claims made by Putin about the atrocities in Ukraine were misrepresentations. According to Paul Roderick Gregory:

> This invisible, clandestine army, toiling away in obscurity, is an indispensable weapon in peddling the Russian narrative of 'neo-Nazi extremists' backed by the U.S. state department and NATO, who usurped control from the 'democratically-elected' Ukrainian

president. We know Putin's visible media and can evaluate it as such. We cannot say the same for Putin's social media warriors, who operate behind a veil of secrecy, anonymity, and assumed identities.[47]

According to alleged reports published in media, Putin used bogus writers and bloggers to post on media sites like Facebook about the crimes and atrocities in Ukraine. Another wing of his campaign used forged photographs of Ukrainian extremists committing crimes. 'Putin awarded medals of the "Order of Service to the Fatherland" to 300 journalists including several editors, directors and television hosts known for their Kremlin-friendly coverage in an executive order signed on 22 April that was not made public,' Alec Luhn expressed in the *Guardian*.[48]

Takeaway

Digital media strategies are used extensively to build brands. The important part of this strategy is to balance a technical support team with concrete messages that can be delivered and shared with the masses.

Some of the important lessons from digital media strategies are:

1. Always speak their language: It is important to speak the language of the voters and to communicate on such platforms with careful and well-versed content.
2. Always play according to budget: Digital strategy is expensive, so it requires scrutiny—which medium would your supporters prefer?
3. Transparency: The AAP followed this effectively. They remained transparent in every single message they

shared online as well as offline. This ensures loyalty and trust.

4. Feedback and criticism: It is said, 'Brave are those who love their enemies.' Digital media platforms are sensitive, and one needs to be very cautious while posting content. In any case if criticism occurs, one needs to accept and correct their mistakes.

5. Innovation: Digital media provides a great opportunity for innovation in content generation, tracking and strategically putting it on other sources.

7

CAMPAIGN FINANCING

Fundraising plays an important role in a candidate's election to public office. Money and politics have been connected since countries started holding elections. In the late 1700s, in the US, only male 'landowners' over the age of twenty-one were allowed to vote, suggesting that you needed financial ground to have your say/opinion.

Two particular foundational circumstances that fuel the development of fundraising are civic volunteerism and progressivism. Civic volunteerism is defined as the willingness to engage in active citizenship by offering time and support to causes and organizations.

However, progressivism can be defined with reference to two actions.

- The power of activism[1]
- Progressives sought to distribute political power directly to citizens through institutions, preventing concentration of wealth and power within the elite.

In the UK, the practice of political donation started with the foundation of the Labour Party. This party sought to mobilize the financial muscle of the working classes through unions so they would be able to compete with older, cadre-style parties. It received donations from trade unions.

In those days, political campaigns required huge amounts of money to be spent on advertising, the cost of transportation, rallies, political consultants, media coverage, etc. The basis of campaign spending depended on the region and the political system. For instance, in the United Kingdom television advertising is provided to campaigning parties for free and it is limited by law. Yet in the United States, it is one of the biggest expenses in the campaign budget, especially for statewide and national campaigns. In India the structure of campaign finance is not well defined. With billions of dollars spent globally on election campaigning, it is now important to analyse where and how parties procure their campaign finances.

Campaign Finance in Action

Common financial sources for political parties include the public purse (subsidies and/or patronage resources), party-run businesses, membership dues and donations from office holders, party members, firms or trade unions.[2] Klaus von Beyme has proposed classifying these sources as internal, external and state support. Many researchers use variants of his categories. 'Internal' funding includes dues and donations from party members, contributions from office holders and funds generated by party enterprises such as newspapers or research services. 'External' funding includes donations from non-members, such as firms, unions and other organizations. 'State support' may include both direct and indirect subsidies, including tax benefits for contributions and the provision of free services.[3]

Fundraising Strategies

Online Fundraising

Digital platforms allow political parties to raise funds through online donations and direct emails. With the world going digital and voters asking for more interactivity with the candidate, campaign committees have started relying heavily on online campaigning. This helps reach people at a large level. The use of social media such as Facebook, Twitter and Google Hangout has been hailed as a successful communication platform because it has increased the donor base.

Obama's campaign team's success in the 2012 presidential elections set an example that other countries could replicate. In 2012, the Obama team raised a whopping $690 million digitally.[4] The Mitt Romney campaign, working in collaboration with the Republican National Committee, raised $182 million online from May 2012 till the election.[5] Over the election cycle of 2014, the Democratic Congressional Campaign Committee (DCCC) raised $171 million as compared to the National Republican Congressional Committee's $131 million. Some attribute this difference in the funds raised by both the parties to the DCCC's use of scare tactics. The DCCC's fundraising emails had subject lines like: 'Painful loss', 'all hope is lost', 'doomed', 'some scary numbers' and, the one that hit the bullseye, 'I will be outspent'.[6] These emails' 'appealing' subject lines convinced people to donate large sums of money right away.

The Obama campaign's social network dashboard organized more than 3,58,000 offline events, increasing the mobility of voters.[7]

In India, the Aam Aadmi Party raised funds through online donations. The party was able to tap into the emotions of common men and women; creating a large base of small-token donors, both inside and outside India. It also launched a mobile app called Aap Ka Daan, making it even easier to donate.

Special Events

Political parties organize events to interact with the voters and raise funds. In the US, fundraising dinners or events are popular among politicians. According to author Brendan J. Doherty, from 2008 to 2012, Obama went to 321 fundraising events.[8] On 21 August 2012, vice-presidential candidate (and Wisconsin Congressman) Paul Ryan attended many high-priced receptions and donor engagements to boost his political bid in the 2012 US elections. His most expensive fundraising dinner was the $50,000 per plate meal at the Union League of Philadelphia.[9]

In India, the Aam Aadmi Party organized a fundraising dinner in Mumbai hosted by Raghu Ram of *MTV Roadies* fame. Each person in attendance was supposed to contribute Rs 20,000 to the party's fund. A similar fundraiser was organized in Bengaluru by the AAP, where people paid to take selfies with Arvind Kejriwal. The trader wing of the AAP organized a fundraising lunch in Delhi, where the party chief promised to rationalize the VAT in Delhi by reducing it on goods that were heavily taxed in comparison to other states, particularly the neighbouring states.[10]

Sale of Campaign Merchandise

Under Chris Hughes's leadership, the Obama campaign team created the brand MyBO or my.barackobama.com with the tagline: 'Keep it real and keep it local'. This tool allowed participants to create their place in the Obama campaign. MyBO featured a variety of ways to contribute and opportunities to purchase campaign merchandise such as bumper stickers, T-shirts, lawn signs, etc. The merchandise flooded the market before the US elections to entice voters. Similarly, Modi launched the NaMo Store (Narendra Modi Store) online to sell merchandise inspired by Modi's life and values.[11] However, BJP denied any fundraising through the popular mode of organizing dinners. In Jammu, BJP launched a special fundraising scheme, announced by the state party president Shamsher Singh Manhas. They called it 'Vishesh Sahyog Nidhi' and 'Aajiwan Sahyog Nidhi' campaigns to raise funds.[12] Like other parties, BJP also has a dedicated online platform for donations. As per Indian Income Tax Act, these donations are exempt from income tax under section 80GGC. In 2013, just before going into nationwide Lok Sabha election of 2014, BJP, with the elected CMs of Madhya Pradesh, Rajasthan, Gujarat, Chhattisgarh and Goa, declared Modi as its prime-ministerial candidate. At the same function, the party also declared 'one vote-one note' campaign based on the old Jan Sangh style of fundraising. People could voluntarily contribute from Rs 10-1000 to party fund. This was the strategy adopted by BJP to connect with the grass-roots voters. Party workers would approach voters to seek donation. Initially, the target was to reach 10 crore families.

8

NEWS MEDIA MANAGEMENT

Narendra Modi and Arvind Kejriwal have both seen the volatile and hostile face of the Indian media. A lot of negative sentiments were expressed but most of them were not backed by facts. The media is playing an ever-increasing role in political campaigning, heavily impacting voters' minds and influencing their decision-making. Sometimes the politician's intentions and even the facts are overshadowed by media hype and negative publicity. Handling the media skilfully is crucial for parties and individuals.

The following matrix shows how a political party can skilfully handle media interaction.

On the y-axis we have societal importance and on the x-axis we have audience interest. Based on the variance of these two variables, different media interaction strategies have been identified. They are as follows:

1. High social importance, high audience interest: mass-market media coverage

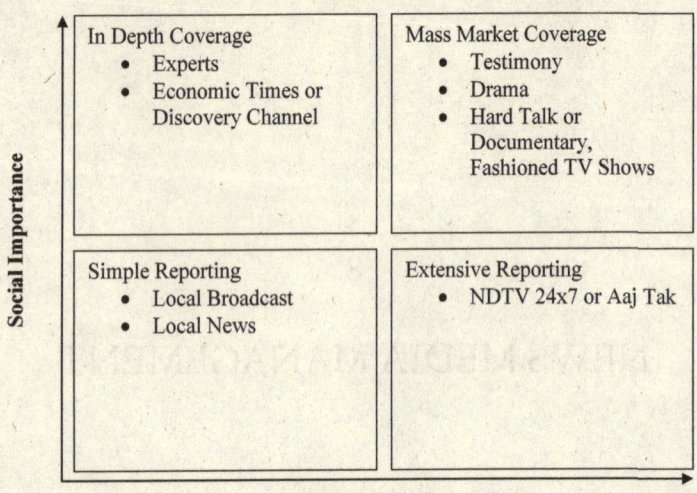

Audience Interest

Source: Sharma, D., 'A Tale of Two Tragedies: Bhopal Gas Leak in India and BP Oil Spill In US', Case Centre, 9 May 2016, MAR0468.

2. High social importance, low audience interest: in-depth coverage
3. Low social importance, high audience interest: extensive reporting
4. Low social importance, low audience interest: simple reporting

From the above discussion, it is clear that media interaction depends on the message being conveyed and the audience's level of interest. No single strategy is perfect in all the scenarios. The conveyed message could range from presenting your views on any issue to negating faulty publicity. Choosing the right platform in media is as important as the message to be conveyed.

News Media Management in Action

Just before the 2014 election, the BJP's prime-ministerial candidate Narendra Modi appeared on a TV programme called *Aap Ki Adalat*. The nation eagerly awaited an interview with Narendra Modi, mostly because they wanted to watch him get grilled by the media. Remarkably, Narendra Modi answered all the questions posed to him in the interview with great ease. As a result, the Modi critics determined that the interview had been fixed; it also seemed that the anchor had posed only easy questions.[1] Despite such criticism, this interview turned into a major image makeover for Modi. He answered every question with utmost confidence and successfully disseminated his message to every section of the society. He assured the minorities that if he became the PM, they would come under no harm. Modi emphasized that his party does not believe in caste politics, stating during his campaign that, 'All are Indians, and all are equal'. He assured the audience that he would institute policies and practices to eradicate corruption from India, promising that the guilty would be punished with a firm hand. While many of Modi's opponents were apprehensive about the idea of their interviews being broadcast nationally, Modi took the opportunity to strengthen his position.[2]

On 27 July 2004, Barack Obama, then a senatorial candidate from Illinois, rose to national prominence after delivering an electrifying speech at the 2004 Democratic National Convention. This speech has come to be regarded as one of 21st century's greatest political speeches. In it he provided a brief family background and conveyed that he was a firm believer of hard work and honesty. He spoke about his connection to America and shared his experience with Americans. On the basis of his speeches, he came to be considered as a man who delivered the right message at the right time. This increased his credibility among the voters.

After this event, Obama reportedly insisted that he only wanted to win the senatorial election and did not have any immediate plans for the presidential election. The political career of Obama took a big jump in the 2004 US senate election. Obama was the first African-American male senator to be elected since Edward Brooke of Massachusetts and the second African-American senator elected from Illinois following Senator Carol Moseley Braun. Jackson stated in his analysis of the 2004 senate election that his status as the only African American in the US senate was enough for Obama to certify his reputation as a political leader. His Democratic National Convention speech delivered in 2004 was extraordinary and helped put him as the front runner for the senate post.[3] However, Obama became the 44th President of the US on 4 November 2008— the first African American to get elected to the nation's highest office. On 6 November 2012, Obama was re-elected to a second term as the President of the United States.

9

WINNING ELECTION THROUGH CAMPAIGN MANAGEMENT

In the 2014 general elections, the Indian public voted against absolute power and rampant corruption by electing Narendra Modi as the prime minister of India. Six months later, Delhi citizens voted against the absolute power of Narendra Modi. This can be viewed as a reaction caused by the fear of BJP's and Modi's perceived monopoly over India's geography.[1] It is evident from the Delhi elections that the idea of one person or party having absolute power does not appeal to the Indian voters any more. India cannot have a Vladimir Putin or the kind of dictatorship communists enjoy in China.

Every election also impacts market sentiments. India's stock market is no exception in this regard. Trading on stock market was marked by extreme volatility as investors tried to gauge the impact of political parties' win or loss.

AAP's stunning victory underlines the change in the meaning of power. Today, the power taken by political parties can no longer exceed what is assigned to them by the electorate.

The power that is given is increasingly contingent in nature and is given when there is sufficient evidence of the office holder's intentions to use it.[2] The victories of Narendra Modi, Arvind Kejriwal and Barack Obama are the victories of leaders as representatives rather than rulers. One of the main causes of the success of Modi, Kejriwal and Obama was their incredible tenacity. They were elected because of the stubborn strain of hope among people that real change is possible.

Winning Election through Campaign Management in Action

Step One: Research and Building Deep Understanding in Action

Every campaign is extraordinary. Therefore, it is very important to completely understand the circumstances and conditions under which your campaign is being conducted and the election will be fought.

Research into the differences and peculiarities of the current situation is the first step towards planning a successful campaign. The initial phase of creating a captivating method must start with a sensible evaluation of the political scene in which one will be contesting.

It is prudent to use components such as the type of election, rules, characteristics of the district, voters, results of the last elections and the weaknesses and strengths of the party's candidate and contestants when planning for election campaigns.

When all this data has been accumulated, one must make a concrete record that will sort the subtle elements into a concrete design that can then be utilized in writing the campaign plan. Today, there are many agencies that provide detailed analysis of voter insights that could help build the reputation for contesting parties.

Grass-roots level agendas that directly connect with people need to be addressed as a priority. During the election campaigns, the BJP concentrated on their plans for initiating Clean Ganga plan, setting up national optic-fibre network at village level and Wi-Fi zones in public areas, bringing back black money, abrogating Article 370 in J&K, formulating an e-governance plan, revamping Public Distribution System, transforming the Food Corporation of India (FCI), building 100 Smart Cities and instituting an all-women mobile bank. At the same time, the AAP promised Jan Lokpal Bill, right to water, full statehood for Delhi and the first corruption-free state of the country.

Step Two: Setting a Clear Objective in Action

A definite objective is necessary in any political battle. Setting objectives is to figure out the tasks that must be carried out to triumph over the opposition. Over and over again, parties neglect to ascertain the number of votes that will be required to ensure triumph and to figure out the origin of these votes. As part of the preliminary research work, one ought to focus on the aggregate populace of a specific region, the aggregate number of voters, casting percentage, votes required to win and the number of households inhabited by voters. A portion of these questions requires some prediction for the future. One must use one's best judgement and compare the current election with past election results.

The BJP and their think tank sent an unambiguous message to supporters and voters that they wanted a clear mandate and not a fragmented one. After all, the party was fighting against the single-party dominance of Congress, which had been in power for sixty years. Setting clear objectives like Mission 272+ was not just a goal to be achieved; it was much larger than that. It emphasized the necessity of a clear majority by any means for a stable government, which can take decisions for the benefit of the citizens. AAP party leader Arvind Kejriwal realized his mistake in last assembly elections after quitting the CM's post. This time, he set a target for five years, 'Paanch Saal Kejriwal'—a message that confers his party power for a complete five years.

Step Three: Segmenting and Targeting Voters in Action

Once a party or politician decides how many votes they need to win, and subsequently the number of voters that need to be encouraged to support their candidate, it is critical to figure out what makes these voters different from those who will not support their candidate. This methodology is called 'targeting voters' or simply 'targeting'.

Targeting should figure out which subgroups of the voting populace are destined to be receptive to the competitor and how one can centre one's own crusade deliberations on these voters.

A lesson from the 2008 US presidential election is applicable here. Obama, with his 'Change' campaign, directly approached the younger population of Americans— especially those aged 18–27. They are active Internet users and have high aspirations. Secondly, with community-based campaigning, he brought locals out for discussion, one-to-one dialogue and idea sharing, making them realize their importance.

In the general elections, the BJP set the target for a clear majority. To achieve a clear mandate, it required proper analysis of its existing strongholds and potential areas of voter segments. In the last general elections, the BJP was reduced to a tally of 116 seats and had not been able to win a majority. Segmenting in an election is largely based on region-wise analysis of voters and the targeting of specific strongholds. For example, the BJP strongholds are in central Indian states like Madhya Pradesh, Gujarat (home state of Narendra Modi) and Chhattisgarh, where the BJP has been in power for the last three terms and had a strong position when it came to voting sentiments. When Modi was appointed the head of the BJP's poll campaign, it struck the right chord with these states, assuring the gathering of major support.

Importance of 'Targeting Voters' in Action

To run a successful campaign, one must conserve the valuable assets of time, cash and individuals, and also create an effective message that will best persuade voters.[3] Targeting voters is important for the following reasons: to save manpower, time and money resources for campaigning, and to create a concrete message that will convince potential voters.

From the point of view of a party, there are three types of voters: supporters, who have chosen to vote in favour of the party, the adversaries' supporters, who have chosen to vote in favour of the party's rivals, and the pool of candidates who have not yet chosen whom to vote for and can still be influenced. In the political arena, these people are termed 'persuadable voters'. The persuadable category of voters needs to be targeted with the correct message.

How to Target Voters?

Establishing the percentage of people who need to be convinced in the electorate requires the evaluation of potential voters and their uniqueness. This can be determined through geographic targeting or figuring out who will vote for your candidate, based on where they live. Another method is demographic targeting, which defines voting populations into different gatherings or subsets of the populace. These delineations can be made based on age, sex, wage, education standard, profession, cultural background or any other distinct characteristic.

In elections, region-based voter targeting is always important. India has diverse voter categories, spread from state to state, region to region, and dominated by local and regional parties (especially in the southern and eastern parts of the country) with high sentiments attached to caste, creed and religion. The BJP, who had lost past elections to regional parties, focused on some crucial states this time, marching their troops into the northern states of UP, Haryana and Bihar. Understanding the importance of voters' sentiments in UP and needing eighty seats from this region, Modi brought his most trusted man, Amit Shah, to conquer the state.

Similarly, the southern parts of India had been challenging for the BJP. They had never been able to get a foothold in these areas due to the strong dominance of local and regional parties. Karnataka was the only state where they had briefly succeeded in the past, and even there they eventually lost their footing due to internal politics. In the southern region, four states account for a total of 129 seats—Karnataka with twenty-eight, Tamil Nadu with thirty-seven, Andhra Pradesh with forty-two and Kerala with twenty. Except for Karnataka, none of these states have any BJP presence. In Andhra Pradesh, the BJP has a good relationship with the local regional party, the Telugu Desam Party (TDP). This alliance benefits both of them and allows them to win a majority of the seats. Similarly, a close alliance with the AIADMK in Tamil Nadu has given the BJP the potential to win a considerable number of votes. Collaborations with major regional and local parties can pay a dividend. The AIADMK won thirty-seven seats out of forty and the TDP won sixteen seats.

Voter Analysis in Action

After deciding an intended target audience for the campaign, it is important to bring them together; the focus should be on values, attitudes, issues and the desire for leadership qualities. In the 2012 US presidential election, an all-electronic campaign management system was used to monitor voters. This electronic campaign management system was by and large a strategic plan to involve young voters across the country in the electoral process. As organizations developed their own systems for data analysis, Obama's team brought in engineers and coders who demonstrated how an election campaign could also be run on a web platform. This was simplified by their extraordinary use of social media, smartphones and advertising. The developers jumped from one state to another, familiarizing themselves with voters and collecting data to convert it into systematic statistical models in an effort to intelligently scrutinize voters.[4]

Voter analysis can be done in reference to statistical data provided by the ECI, e.g., number of parties contesting, registered, recognized and unrecognized; number of electors and percentage of their voting constituency wise, accepted and rejected voting percentage; number of polling stations; and average number of electors per polling station. The ECI reports can be used to analyse various voter segments in different constituencies. The ECI also provides demographic data about the electors. Detailed election results are also available on their website.

Determining Values in Action

Values are determined by knowledge of the interest group's ideologies and intentions. For example, what does a group of supporters value more: social insurance or financial opportunity? Societal responsibility or individual flexibility? Security or peace? Change or police security? What qualities do they impart to the remaining populace? What qualities separate them from the remaining populace?

The BJP has always been viewed as the political arm of the RSS, which is considered to be a right-wing organization. When it comes to developing agendas, image and support, the BJP, to some extent, derives its ideology from the RSS. In Gujarat, Narendra Modi is himself a brand. He created a legacy and made Gujarat a role model for good governance. In the last fifteen years, Modi has ensured that his government delivers every promise that has been made for the betterment of the people of the state. He promised around-the-clock electricity, an e-governance model, an amicable atmosphere for businesses, departments working without hassle and the participation of NRIs and FDI in investments through programmes like 'Vibrant Gujarat'. The major focuses of his government were economic development, job creation through skill-oriented education and working for technological innovation. The simple philosophy that Modi used in promoting Gujarat was economic freedom.

In the Delhi assembly elections, the AAP and Arvind Kejriwal had a tough time. Though they won the mandate in the last election and formed the government, they quickly lost their focus and Kejriwal resigned from the CM's post after only forty-nine days. In the most recent election, the party realized its mistake and apologized to voters.

They realized that voters' sentiments were still with them, and it had been the party's core values that had brought them in power six months ago. Delhi politicians had a reputation for corruption and not fulfilling promises. This, along with the security of women, has also been a major concern of the state. Kejriwal asked voters to believe in their efforts to make the capital a corruption-free state. His mantra for voters to rely on was 'Swaraj'. The AAP's vision document states, '[D]ream of SWARAJ that Gandhi had envisaged for a free India—where the power of governance and rights of democracy will be in the hands of the people of India.'[5]

Similarly, Obama's US presidential election campaign was very different from that of his predecessors. Barack Obama consistently talked about bringing about a change in the culture of US elections. At the time of the election, US economy was in a shambles. Obama emphasized economic reforms in the form of tax relief, support for education and technological innovation. His dream was to ensure healthcare for all US citizens. He also promised to bring back the troops that had been deployed after 9/11 as soon as possible.

Attitudes in Action

Voter attitudes are crucial to the future, whether they are idealistic or sceptical. Voters' opinions, beliefs, states of mind, thinking processes and their needs are key attitudinal factors.

Change in attitude requires much effort, not just towards policymaking and luring the voters with big promises but also in focusing on legitimate and relevant issues that help create a positive attitude towards one's candidate or party. The party should have a positive attitude. They have to make their supporters believe that only they can bring about the necessary changes. A good example of this is the BJP's efforts in setting up a positive attitude. Today in India, when we talk about growth, prosperity, security for masses, business friendliness and economic freedom, we immediately talk about Gujarat. The entrepreneurial nature of the Gujarati people and their willingness to innovate in business helped them achieve their goals. The effort of the government, the people, the industry and the strong NRI population of Gujaratis around the globe transformed the attitude of negative emotions into positive ones.

In a corruption-riddled country where the Congress and its leaders have been at the centre of these allegations, Modi's impeccable integrity shines. He has focused his energy on making Gujarat an example of notable administration and good governance. He has achieved phenomenal development and economic growth and at the same time bolstered social inclusiveness. He has worked hard to regain the confidence of the minorities, even as the relentless and pervasive campaigning against him has continued unabated on electronic media among intellectuals and civil society activists.

Issues in Action

One must know about the imperative issues, like those involving money, social issues and foreign policy, that make voters sit up and pay attention to the general elections. The

2014 general elections were different in many ways to previous Indian elections. For many years, elections were fought on the grounds of the welfare of marginalized sections of the country, poverty, agricultural issues, backward and tribal classes and religion. From the Nehruvian era to Indira Gandhi's regime to Narasimha Rao's government's revival policies, elections have been fought on similar grounds. In 1996, when Vajpayee formed the first non-Congress government, issues shifted from conventional grounds to more modern agendas—like India Shining, GDP, economic growth and bilateral issues.

The 2014 election was different because the rampant corruption prevailing in all sections of government caused widespread protests. The issue of corruption caused national unrest, courtesy Anna Hazare and Arvind Kejriwal. Corruption and the resultant numerous scams and scandals invariably led to inflation. Common men and women succumbed due to the high inflation of basic goods like vegetables, grains, sugar and other commodities.

High inflation rates added to the issue of unemployment. Indian youth felt the heat as unemployment among the young rose. According to the Census of 2011, India's working-age population (aged 15–64 years) is 63.4 per cent of the total population. By 2020, India is poised to become world's youngest nation, with an average age of twenty-nine years. If the country wants to enjoy the maximum benefit of this surplus then they have to create jobs and provide education and skills to become competent. The young population, aged 21–35, was not content with the governmental policies of the time. This led to poor economic performance, the lowest GDP rate in the last five years and rising fiscal deficit; balance of payments put pressure on the already suffocating economy. The poor were getting poorer and the rich were getting richer.

Women's safety was another issue, which struck a blow to the previous government. People felt unsafe and helpless. Rising tensions with Pakistan after the killing of an Indian soldier at the border and China's policies also frightened voters.

These issues brought a silver lining for the regional parties. After the fall of Congress, many small- and medium-sized parties tried to get into the mainstream. Although the BJP reaped the biggest rewards from this turmoil, every citizen fought against it. Some regional party leaders like J. Jayalalithaa, Nitish Kumar, Naveen Patnaik and Mamata Banerjee raised the issue of social empowerment.

Leadership Qualities in Action

Leaders of Today Will Be Leaders for Tomorrow

Voters look out for which qualities in their leaders? Are they searching for steady, accomplished authority or do they want a youthful, dynamic and charismatic person ready to fight against conventions? Are they inclined towards pioneers from the intellectual elite or do they need pioneers who can identify with the apprehensions of the common people?

One needs to accomplish certain clear and defined requirements in order to become a professional like lawyer, teacher, doctor or administrative officer, but to become a political leader, one might need to be elusive. Being a politician requires certain areas of expertise, and one must be distinctive. Communication is integral to strong political leadership. Politicians are the ones who tell the masses that they will support them. A good political leader must be able to build a road map—full of new plans and initiatives—which goes according to the party's agenda. Another component of successful political leadership is 'energy', the never-dying attitude of let's-go-for-another-rally and the ability to handle pressure, extremism and criticism. The appropriate word for this is courageousness.

In politics, the ability to judge a future course of action or trend is far more important than making a bold decision. Those who possess this skill are the darlings of their leadership and inspire natural respect. Some components of successful political leadership can be summarized in the following manner:

1. Integrity and loyalty towards supporters, followers and their party organization
2. Interpersonal skills and concrete communication, specific to an agenda
3. Willingness to sacrifice
4. A distinguished character
5. Ability to take a stand
6. Willingness to make strong decisions

An effective political leader is able to stand up and take responsibility, accepting his or her flaws with the clear ambition of working for the people. This requires a certain level of accountability and the ability to admit the truth. Leadership also requires a certain level of competence. One must have the underlying characteristics that are required to perform a given task or activity, or play a role with desired success. This can be generic knowledge, reason, personality or tangible skills related to higher job performance. Management theory divides competency into four areas:

1. Managerial: Ability with skills required to plan, organize and mobilize resources

2.   Human: Development of knowledge, attitudes and skills
     to motivate human resources
3.   Conceptual: Thinking beyond the obvious and at an
     abstract level
4.   Functional: Educational background and technical
     expertise in a specific role

We surveyed a random sample of 385[6] (210 male and 175
female) residents of Delhi using the mall-intercept method.[7] If
they could, participants were asked to fill out questionnaires,
and data collators explained the survey in Hindi to those who
could not understand it. Leader competency was rated on
a scale of 1 to 8, with 1 denoting 'very poor' and 8 denoting
'exceptional' leadership. The results of the survey are presented
in the following table:

Competency	Kiran Bedi	Arvind Kejriwal	Ajay Maken	Narendra Modi
Managerial	4.0	5.5	5.2	7.2
Human	4.0	5.5	4.2	7.4
Functional	5.5	5.8	4.8	4.1
Conceptual	3.0	5.4	4.6	7.0

Source: Delhi assembly elections of 2014: survey conducted for
major candidates of two national and one regional party: Kiran Bedi
(BJP), Ajay Maken (Congress) and Arvind Kejriwal (AAP).[8]

The results show that Kejriwal secured higher rating than
his main competitor, the BJP's candidate, Bedi. Modi,
who had just become the prime minister of India, almost
outscored all the candidates in popular perception of
competency.

Step Four: Creating the Campaign Message in Action

A campaign message must be concrete in nature. Once a target group is identified, the message needs to be delivered to them with sincerity. It is not only a message, but a dialogue between the candidate and the voters that is filled with intensity and purpose. A party's message determines its ability to contest and becomes the basis for potential voters to decide if they will vote for it.

A campaign message is not the candidate's projection of what he or she will do if chosen, it is not a rundown on the issues the candidate will address and it is not a straightforward appealing expression or trademark. These can all be a part of a campaign message but they must not be mistaken for the message itself, which is a basic articulation that will be rehashed again and again throughout the duration of the elections in an effort to influence the targeted voters.

A message should be concise, straight and valid. It should come from the qualities, practices, policies and experiences of a candidate. It cannot conflict with the competitor's experience. Likewise, the message ought to be conceivable. Competitors who make doubtful guarantees induce voter disregard. Voters must accept what you are saying about yourself and what your intentions are, so the message has to be genuine. It is therefore paramount to reinforce your announcements with confirmation of experience or learning from your past.

A message should be convincing and it should seem important to voters. You must discuss subjects that are essential to your intended interest group. These subjects should be issues that voters face daily in their lives, not issues that legislators think are essential to public policy. Voters are more prone to help candidates who discuss their occupations, their children's education or their benefits than the candidates who discuss the budget, despite the fact that the budget will influence these things, i.e. if you are trying to persuade voters that you are the only suitable contender to speak for them in an effort to gain their votes then communication needs to be properly designed.

A campaign message should be equipped with clarity and speak to the heart. The message should be delivered in a dialect that enables voters to accept and understand it effectively. To impress voters, government officials perpetually use specialized words that the voters either do not comprehend or do not find significant. It is much better to craft a visual picture in their minds. Discussions of individuals, things and real-life circumstances to depict conceptual thoughts, for example, financial strategy, should take place. Governments promote their policies through advertisements. These advertisements largely talk about the change a policy has made in the lives of people. But, these promotions are limited to the populist programmes. In case of budgets and financial plans, a large proportion of population is not aware of plans, policies and provisions. It is very important for a government to disseminate financial plans to every citizen to make it beneficial and inclusive. Politics, by and large, is a game of emotions and legislators who engage the minds and hearts of voters generally defeat individuals who appeal to their heads.

One must figure out how to address voters' core values and signal that one is deeply concerned with the issues that they confront every day. Campaign messages need to be dynamic, meaning they should be easy to alter according to the situation, location and overall environment. When it's clear what message will influence a candidate's target voters, they must repeat that same message at each open door. Though there is no way to guarantee voter attention, giving an effective campaigning message, repeatedly in distinctive ways, will usually interest voters.

Credibility in Action: Building Your Credibility and Downgrading Your Opponents'

When a campaign message is being considered, even the minutest details must be prioritized in an effort to target more voters than the opposition. There are two approaches to influencing the greatest number of voters. First, one can do and say things to boost their credibility, focusing on one's positive qualities and highlighting one's famous opinions. Second, one can attempt to deflate the tall claims made by his or her rival. This can be done by calling attention to what voters will see as your rival's negative characteristics or unpopular stances on issues.

Out of the two systems, which you pick and in what blend frequently relies upon what position you end up in throughout the span of the fight. These two approaches independently and combined together decide the position of your stance in the campaign. The campaigner has to choose carefully what he is going to say about himself and what image he wants to create of his opponent in the minds of voters. There is no point in attacking your opponent so much that people start seeing you as a negative campaigner. If you are leading in surveys and feel optimistic about your chances to win effectively, then you can focus on increasing your credibility. Yet if you are behind in the surveys, increasing your credibility may not be sufficient to win. For this situation, you may need to raise your credibility and, in the meantime, work to counter the tall and false claims made by your rivals.

US Presidential Election in Action

In Bill Clinton's 1992 US presidential campaign, his challenge to George Bush exemplified credibility building. This presidential battle is still regarded as one of the strongest in terms of conveying a successful message reliably, time and again.

Clinton's message was simple:[9] After twelve years of Republican leadership resulting in social stagnation and economic recession, the American people are ready for change. The choice in 1992 was clear: change or more of the same.[10] This small message was honest, believable and imperative to a dominant segment of voters. It was targeted at those among the middle class and workers who were not happy with Republican policies. In fact, all the campaigns of Clinton were attached with 'change or more of the same' message. The message was designed to target a specific audience: specialists and the white-collar workers who felt that the Republican approach was not helping them excel.

Another incredible political speaker in US politics is President Barack Obama. By communicating a message of 'progress' and 'trust', Obama caught the creative energy of many American voters, including the youth. Through compelling utilization of a decentralized campaign and solid web coverage, the Obama campaign took its message of progress to voters on a phenomenal scale. His main sentiments were 'change we can believe in' and the trademark 'Yes, we can.'

The following speech by Obama[11] on election night, 4 November 2008, demonstrates this skill:

> If there is anyone out there who still doubts that America is a place where all things are possible, who still wonders if the dream of our founders is alive in our time, who still questions the power of our democracy, tonight is your answer. It's the answer told by lines that stretched around schools and churches in numbers this nation has never seen, by people who waited three hours and four hours, many for the very first time in their lives, because they believed that this time must be different, that their voice could be that difference.
>
> Yes, we can.
>
> This is our chance to answer that call. This is our moment. This is our time—to put our people back to work and open doors of opportunity for our kids, to restore prosperity and promote the cause of peace, to reclaim the American dream and reaffirm that fundamental truth—that out of many, we are one, that while we breathe, we hope, and where we are met with cynicism and doubt, and those who tell us that we can't, we will respond with that timeless creed that sums up the spirit of a people:
>
> Yes, we can.
>
> Thank you. God bless you, and may God bless the United States of America.[12]

Obama's DNC speech on Tuesday, 27 July, 2004, is considered to be one of the best speeches of twenty-first century. It was a call to voters, especially those in the younger generation, to make the most important decision of their lives, the decision for 'change'. He asked voters to make a difference with their voice. Obama framed the speech around the huge challenges that are faced by common Americans: jobs, social security, health security and new threats. The change Obama promised was a revamping of the age-old system of politics that had led to economic crisis and unemployment. He reminded them of the pillars of American society: democracy, liberty, opportunity and unyielding hope. The connection was obvious as he promised honesty, peace and security. He reminded them that it was the right time to reclaim the American dream and reaffirm the fundamental truth, imploring them to stand united.

Step Five: Media Management in Action

Politics and elections are important occasions that attract more media attention than most other events. Parties can use daily papers, TV, Internet and radio to get their campaign messages out. However, this requires a good relationship with news people, a convincing motivation in sharing their story and an effectively comprehended point to their message. Nowadays, various parties appoint a dedicated staff of press secretaries who manage the majority of press and media-related work.

There are two reasons why it is important for each party to maintain a good rapport with the print and broadcast community. First, whenever a writer prints or telecasts a tale about election battle, the message goes directly to the intended audience free of cost. This is particularly valid regarding free political weeklies and the majority of the web news sites. Further, the substitutes (like official party newsletter, publication, speeches delivered at public functions and rallies) of media are regularly viewed as invalid. Electorates are substantially more inclined to accept positive data about a politician if it originates from an 'autonomous' source, like a mass telecast rather than from a 'one-sided' source, like the party's campaign.

Press conferences must be well planned and should be important enough for press reporters to attend so they can gather meaningful information. The party should furnish the press with a photograph of the candidate, profiles, written material, applicable position papers, press clippings and statements that the party wants to release. It is very important that every time a party organizes a press conference, they also try to strengthen their overall communication and relationship with the media community.

One cannot only depend on columnists for the publicity required for the campaign. The party may also need to buy extra attention from daily papers and radio or TV commercials. Yet media management can go wrong and have a negative impact. During an interview with NDTV's Ravish Kumar on 27 January 2015, the BJP's Delhi chief-ministerial candidate Kiran Bedi not only tried to avoid questions but actually tried to run away. Though it was a pre-election interview and should have been handled carefully, Bedi came off as hurried and did not seem keen to answer all of the journalist's questions. She began avoiding questions and literally ran away from a media person. This created a negative buzz around her in the media almost immediately. After this debacle, some of the leaders from rival parties suggested that she appoint a media manager, exposing her weakness.[13]

Social Media Management in Action

Social networks are new stages for trading individual and professional data. Discussion platforms on social media like Facebook, Twitter and LinkedIn have been used in a large way to collect data about political campaigns, voters and leaders. It needs to be understood that the Internet only provides an inert source of communication, meaning that it does not go to the voters; the voters need to come to it. Personal web pages are definitely a powerful tool for communication. If it is well supported by the Internet users, it instantly gets connected to the largest network globally. It is interactive and available at all times. These web pages provide personal and professional information about the person. That makes them appealing to the supporters. Many leaders share images, videos and daily updates.

The effective use of social networking in the US presidential elections has made Twitter, Facebook, MySpace and other social networking integral parts of the political campaigning toolkit. Few researchers give online campaigning enough credit for Obama's victory. Obama's personal communication site, my.barackobama.com, helped him set records as far as donations and grass-roots mobilization were concerned[14].

Agenda Setting in Action

Agenda setting is one of the most important parts of any election campaign. Entman[15] argues that 'to frame is to select some aspects of a perceived reality and make them more salient in a communicating text, in such a way as to promote a particular problem definition, causal interpretation, moral evaluation, and/or treatment recommendation for the item described.'

The power of the media is that it influences the presentation of requests in news reports about events and issues related to the masses. Media uses different models to prioritize the agendas. In the bottom-up model of agenda setting, media focuses more on public's concerns. These public concerns are then posited to influence political agenda. The other approach is top-down model, where political discourse influences media's agenda.[16] There are two levels of agenda setting. On the first level, the media uses interesting and leading objects or issues to impact the general public's thinking. In the second stage, the media emphasizes the legitimacy of issues, like what would people be thinking. Agenda setting theory helps create apolitical ads, campaigns, business news, public relations, etc.

Agenda setting is primarily related to gatekeeping. It controls the choice of matter debated by the media. Normally, people think generally about the consequences of a media gatekeeping. It is particularly editors who are the media's watchmen. News media chooses what occasions to publicize on the grounds of their 'newsworthiness'.[17]

Step Six: Volunteer Management in Action

In creating your voter contact plan, you must understand that you cannot finish everything with only the few individuals who began helping on the campaign. To run a successful election campaign, you will need people whom you may not be able to pay. This is the place where volunteers become necessary. As your campaign starts convincing voters that you are the best competitor, it will likely draw in individuals who will offer considerably more help than their vote. These individuals will need to volunteer in the campaign and support you till you win.

Individuals volunteer for many reasons. The primary volunteers are frequently party followers who want to be included for a sense of commitment. Some individuals volunteer because they feel firmly about a specific issue—they either admire your stance or strongly disagree with your competitors'. Some individuals are simply social and want to be included in the political fight to spend time with friends or other people who share their interests. Some individuals volunteer because they see it as a chance to get a job. Finally, some individuals volunteer because they are looking for acknowledgement.

Volunteers stay with campaigns if they feel that they are making a commitment, if they feel acknowledged, if they feel that the work is intriguing, if they are meeting interesting individuals or if the work is fun. Volunteers can be highly dedicated, but if they are putting in an excessive amount of work, it increases the chances that they will leave the battle because they are exhausted or feel that the work they have been given will not make any difference.

Volunteers can come from numerous distinctive zones. The principal volunteers will presumably be companions of the candidate and activists who have helped with past campaigns. These volunteers will likely not be enough to perform all of the campaign's work, and more individuals will need to be discovered. You ought to search for individuals who have volunteered in different areas of their lives.

They may volunteer for community associations, neighbourhood aggregates, religious associations, unions, schools and so forth. Your campaign message should address a specific issue or gathering, and you must be ready to convince associations working towards particular issues to help you and encourage more volunteer participation. As your campaign moves forward to voters, you ought to take each chance to ask individuals to help in the campaign.

Step Seven: Managing Public Relations in Action

The field of public relations involves dealing with and disseminating precise and relevant data to the general society.

This function is particularly critical to election officials as they need to verify the voters and have the actual data. They are required to participate effectively in the decision-making process and have an important role in exercising and incorporating teachings, illuminating all the clients and counting candidates, elected officials, media, voters, staff and the overall population.

To educate the general society, it is fundamental for decision-making authorities and the media to cooperate to communicate the exact data about voting procedures. It is important when working with columnists to get data to the public through election offices spread across the country. Election officials must strive to create cost-effective activities to guarantee that the general population comprehends the organization of elections and is above all educated about how to take part in the electoral race.

Public relations have a very significant impact on voters. The efforts invested in improving public relations will affect a voter's capacity to comprehend and take part in the decision process. It is a good idea to use mailings to inform voters on how to stamp their vote and to post this information at surveying areas. Give simple instructions under big headings on the best way to utilize voting gear and how to check a poll. Post this data in extensive (very large in quantity, on a large scale) print inside places where voters are surveyed and where they stand in line at voting stations.

Create a website for your election office. If you need assets to achieve this, consider banding together with other neighbourhood election offices within your state or with your state decision office to create a statewide website. The web page must be open for business twenty-four hours a day, seven days a week, so you need the technical capability to have many guests. Use this media to teach and advise everybody, including voters, candidates, chosen officials, media, survey workers, students and so on.

Step Eight: Booth Management in Action

All of the efforts that you have put into campaigning and contesting elections should ideally culminate in people coming out to polling booths to vote. If you want to win an election, you must focus on winning each booth in your constituency. This requires a lot of strategizing and delicate execution. A well-received campaign can result in disappointment if your booths are not managed appropriately.

A detailed map showing all the booths of your constituency is necessary. You must be aware of each booth's total population, its demographic composition and your target population segments. Based on this data, you need to assign an adequate number of volunteers to manage each booth. The BJP's victory in the 2014 general elections can be attributed to their 'one booth ten youth' (or twenty youth in UP) strategy. This plan was executed with full precision and resulted in a resounding victory.

It is important that volunteers reach out to the voting population on the day of polling or on the night before, reminding them to come out and vote for you. The volunteers also need to ensure that the voters who stay away from their constituencies travel back to their constituency a day before to cast their vote. Appropriate arrangements should be made to ensure that the elderly and first-time voters are properly assisted and brought to the polling booths.

Volunteers assigned to the polling booths should be alert enough to prevent fraudulent voting and report any unfair practices. They should be able to identify the voters and give them their election slips (voter identification card that carries their name and identity number). They need to guide the voters to the appropriate polling booths. First-time voters need to be educated on the polling process and how to use the electronic voting machines.

In a nutshell, booth management is done by a self-guided army of volunteers, who ensure your electoral victory. It is essential that this team is composed of experienced and capable members. This group has to be motivated and equipped with the tools and techniques to handle the election process.

To ensure a high voter turnout, the BJP instituted a strategy that aggressively involved its volunteers, who went to the doorsteps of voters when there was just around one hour till the end of polling. The panna pramukh (in charge of a page of around 1100 electoral rolls) had been tasked with reaching out to at least thirty voters. Over one lakh volunteers, several of them affiliated with the RSS, visited around 12,000 polling stations across Delhi. The panna pramukh strategy was part of BJP President Amit Shah's micromanagement strategy at the booths in an effort to ensure that no stone was left unturned at a grass-roots level.

This strategy was adopted from the RSS. The BJP created an army of panna prabhaaris (page heads, also called panna pramukhs)[18] in UP to focus on approximately sixty voters per panna prabhaari. Each prabhaari was given responsibility for a panna—which literally means a page, but in this case referred to a page in the electoral rolls. Each page in the voters' list has the names of eight to twelve families. Each panna prabhaari was required to focus on these families. The impact of the strategy was immediate and immense. It worked excellently to mobilize voters.

Another interesting feature of this plan is the fact that it engaged as many people as possible in the greater cause. As per the BJP team, not all the panna prabhaaris were RSS workers. Many of them joined the movement because they had genuine expectations from the new regime.

The Road Ahead

A major chunk of political aspirants across the globe are desirous of imperium. In recent times, the road to contest and win state and national assembly elections is laden with micromanaging each and every aspect of citizen's lives.

Rising corporate participation in election process has advanced the trend towards competitive primaries.

Though we know suffrage is unique power wielded by citizens, their united decision to seek out candidates who support their issues is influenced by exposure to conscious as well as unconscious exposure to multifaceted PR campaigns of political parties. The fine balance between power and responsibility of both the party and public is the will to create a union built on the fundamental that a nation is strongest when it's united through its citizens; when all work together to accomplish a better standard of living for all.

ACKNOWLEDGEMENTS

I wish to express my gratitude to my research associates and interns at IIM-Ahmedabad. Particularly, I wish to thank Yogesh Atray, Neha, Gaurav, Shivangee, Namrata, Anshita, Dishant and Mehak for their help during the writing of this book.

NOTES

Chapter 1: Campaign Management and Its Importance

1. Westcott, Kathryn, 'Bush Revels in Cowboy Speak', BBC News, 6 June 2003, http://news.bbc.co.uk/2/hi/americas/2968176. stm.
2. Rodgers, Walter, 'John Wayne President Has Critics', CNN.com, 30 January 2003, https://web.archive.org/ web/20080907203320/http:/www.cnn.com/2003/WORLD /europe/01/30/europe.bush.rodgers.otsc.
3. Westcott, Kathryn, 'Bush Revels in Cowboy Speak', BBC News, 6 June 2003, http://news.bbc.co.uk/2/hi/americas/2968176. stm.
4. Gundalach, G.T., 'AMA Committee on Definitions', *Marketing Definitions: A Glossary of Marketing Terms*, Chicago: AMA,1960, http://www.unf.edu/~ggundlac/pdfs/pub_10.pdf.
5. Kotler, Philip and Levy, Sidney J., 'Broadening the Concept of Marketing', *Journal of Marketing* 33, January 1969, pp. 10–15.
6. Kotler, Philip, 'A Generic Concept of Marketing', *Journal of Marketing* 36, April 1972, pp. 46–54.
7. Plasser, Fritz and Plasser, Gunda, *Global Political Campaigning: A Worldwide Analysis of Campaign Professionals and Their Practices*, Westport, CT: Praeger, 2002.

8. Blumler, Jay G., 'Elections, the Media and the Modern Publicity Process', *Public Communication: The New Imperatives: Future Directions for Media Research*, ed. Marjorie Ferguson, Thousand Oaks: Sage, 1990, pp. 101–13.

9. Kavanagh, Dennis, 'New Campaign Communications: Consequences for British Political Parties', *The Harvard International Journal of Press/Politics* 1:3, 1996, pp. 60–76.

10. Plasser and Plasser, *Global Political Campaigning*.

11. Blumler, J.G. and Kavanagh, D., 'The Third Age of Political Communication: Influence and features', *Political Communication* 16(3), 1999, pp. 209-230.

12. Butler, David, Penniman, Howard R. and Ranney, Austin, *Democracy at the Polls: A Comparative Study of Competitive National Elections*, Washington, D.C., American Enterprise Institute for Public Policy Research, 1981.

13. Norris, P., 'The Evolution of Election Campaigns: Eroding Political Engagement?', Political Communications in the 21st Century, Otago, New Zealand, 2004.

14. Bhowmick, N. and Thottam, J., 'India's Anticorruption Activist Ready to End Fast—with a Few Conditions', Time. com, 26 August 2011, http://content.time.com/time/world/article/0,8599,2090562,00.html.

15. 'FAQs—Election Machinery', Election Commission of India, 15 February 2015, http://eci.nic.in/eci_main1/election-machinery.aspx.

16. Kondo, N., 'Election Studies in India', Institute of Developing Economies, JETRO, Chiba, March 2007.

17. Adolphsen, M., 'Branding in Election Campaigns: Just a Buzzword or a New Quality of Political Communication', LSE, 2009, http://www.lse.ac.uk/media@lse/research/mediaWorkingPapers/MScDissertationSeries/Past/Adolphsen_final.pdf.

18. 'Amendments Made under 42nd Constitutional Amendment Act', UPSCGuide.com, 15 February 2016, http://www.upscguide.com/content/ammendments-made-under-42nd-constitutional-amendment-act.

19. Anuja, 'Bihar Still Votes on Identity Lines', Livemint, 13 April 2014, http://www.livemint.com/Politics/bST8VvV3PLwQoJdLvY63dP/Bihar-still-votes-on-identitylines.html.

20. 'Mamata Banerjee: It's a Victory for "Maa, Maati, Manush"', *Economic Times*, 13 May 2011, http://articles.economictimes. indiatimes.com/2011-05-13/news/29540222_1_ mamatabanerjee-trinamool-congress-west-bengal.

21. Express News Service, 'On Last Day of Campaigning, Modi Plays Gujarati Pride Card', *Indian Express*, 29 April 2014, http://indianexpress.com/article/cities/ahmedabad/on-last-day-ofcampaigning-modi-plays-gujarati-pride-card.

22. Björkman, Lisa, '"Vote Banking" as Politics in Mumbai', *Patronage as Politics in South Asia*, ed. Anastasia Piliavsky, Delhi: Cambridge University Press, 2014, pp. 176.

23. Manivannan, R., '1991 Tamil Nadu Elections: Issues, Strategies and Performance', *Economic and Political Weekly*, 1992, pp. 164–70.

24. '90% Indians Vote on Caste Lines, Says Katju', *The Hindu*, 31 March 2013, http://www.thehindu.com/news/national/other-states/90-indians-vote-on-caste-lines-says katju/article4564972.ece.

25. Long, D.J., 'The Determinants of Ethnic Voting', Harvard Academy of International and Area Studies, University of Washington, 2012, http://cega.berkeley.edu/assets/miscellaneous_files/Long_WG APE101112.pdf.

26. 19 Election Commission of India, 10 March 2015, http://eci.nic.in/eci/eci.html.

27. TNN, 'Contrasting Voting Pattern in Indore-5', *Times of India*, 26 November 2013, http://articles.timesofindia.indiatimes.com/2013-11-26/madhya-pradesh-assemblyelections/44487802_1_booths-polling-stations-votingpattern.

28. Duggal, A., Chauhan, A., Tibrewala, M., Ahmed, T., 'To identify the drivers behind a voter's purchase decision; implications for

political marketing campaigns in the context of Aam Aadmi Party', IIMA project for Talent Management Course, 2015.

29. Plasser and Plasser, *Global Political Campaigning*.

30. Ibid.

31. Ibid.

32. PTI, 'Lok Sabha Elections 2014 Pegged as Most Expensive Polls with Government Spending a Whopping Rs 3,426 crores', *DNA*, 13 May 2014, http://www.dnaindia.com/india/report-lok-sabha-elections-2014-pegged-as-mostexpensive-polls-with-government-spending-a-whopping-rs-3426-crores-1987859.

33. Bemoneyaware.com, 4 April 2014, http://www.bemoneyaware.com/blog/cost-of-india-loksabha-elections-2014/#more-10785.

34. Huilgol, Mahit, 'Total Number of Permitted TV Channels in India as of July is 798, I&B Ministry Gives Clearance to 3 New Channels', Telecomtalk.info, 5 August 2014, http://telecomtalk.info/total-number-of-tv-channels-in-india-as-ofjuly798/120527.

35. Chandrashekhar, Vaishnavi, 'A Dab of Primary Colors in India's "Americanized" Election', *Christian Science Monitor*, 9 April 2014, http://www.csmonitor.com/World/Asia-South-Central/2014/0409/A-dab-of-primary-colors-in-India-s-Americanized-election-video.

36. Chakravarty, Praveen, 'Case for Candidate Primaries for Elections', *Outlook India*, 5 October 2015, http://www.outlookindia.com/website/story/case-for-candidateprimaries-for-elections/295507.

Chapter 2: Campaign Management: Star Campaigner

1. Unnithan, Chitra, '4Ps of Marketing Helped Modi Become Prime Minister: Study', *Times of India*, 30 May 2014, http://timesofindia.indiatimes.com/india/4Ps-of-marketing-helped-Modi-become-Prime-Minister-Study/articleshow/35741339.cms.

2. Berreby, David, 'A Real-life Version of the Hitler's Sweater Experiment', BigThink.com, 15 February 2016, http://bigthink. com/Mind-Matters/a-real-life-version-of-the-hitlerssweater-experiment.

3. Blumer, Herbert, 'Collective Behavior', A. M. Lee, ed., *Principles of Sociology*, New York: Barnes & Noble, 1951, pp. 67–121.

4. Sager, Ryan, 'Do Celebrity Endorsements Work?', MarketWatch. com, 21 March 2011, http://www.marketwatch.com/story/ docelebrity-endorsements-work-1300481444531.

5. Erdogan, B.Z., 'Celebrity Endorsement: A Literature Review', *Journal of Marketing Management* 15: 4, 1999, pp. 291–314.

6. McCracken, G., 'Who Is the Celebrity Endorser? Cultural Foundations of the Endorsement Process', *Journal of Consumer Research*, 1989, pp. 310–21.

7. Mukherjee, Debiprasad, 'Impact of Celebrity Endorsements on Brand Image', 6 August 2009, http://ssrn.com/abstract=1444814 or http://dx.doi.org/10.2139/ssrn.1444814.

8. Garthwaite, C. and Moore, T.J., 'Can Celebrity Endorsements Affect Political Outcomes? Evidence from the 2008 US Democratic Presidential Primary', *Journal of Law, Economics, and Organization*, 2013, http://jleo.oxfordjournals.org/content/ early/2012/02/10/jleo.ewr031.abstract.

9. Mukherjee, J., 'The Impact of Celebrity Endorsement on Brand Image', Social Science Research Network, 4 August 2009, http://dx.doi.org/10.2139/ssrn.1444814.

10. Adolphsen, M., 'Branding in Election Campaigns: Just a Buzzword or a New Quality of Political Communication?', LSE, 2009, http:// www.lse.ac.uk/media@lse/research/mediaWorkingPapers/ MScDissertationSeries/Past/Adolphsen_final.pdf.

11. Micheletti, M. and Stolle, D., 'The Concept of Political Consumerism', *Youth Activism—an International Encyclopedia*, ed. L.R. Sherrod, Westport: Greenwood Publishing, 2005.

12. Burkitt, Catherine, 'Are You Less Emotionally Intelligent than Blair? And If So Why Should You Care?', Political Studies Association, Aberdeen, UK, 2002.

13. Scammell, M., 'Political Brands and Consumer Citizens: The Rebranding of Tony Blair', *Annals of the American Academy of Political and Social Science* 611:1, 2007, pp. 176–92.

14. Dawar, N. and Bagga, C.K., 'A Better Way to Map Brand Strategy', *Harvard Business Review*, June 2015, https://hbr.org/2015/06/a-better-way-to-map-brand-strategy.

15. Kumar, R., 'Shotgun May Lose Star Campaigner Tag', *Hindustan Times*, 30 August 2015, http://www.pressreader.com/india/hindustan-times-patiala/20150830.

16. Parvatiyar, Deepak, 'Political Campaigns and Elections in India', Elections.in, 12 September 2014, http://www.elections.in/blog/political-campaigns-and-elections-in-india.

17. Chhibber, Pradeep, K. and Ostermann, Susan L., 'The BJP's Fragile Mandate: Modi and Vote Mobilizers in the 2014 General Elections', *Studies in Indian Politics* 2:2, 2014, pp. 137–51, http://inp.sagepub.com/content/2/2/137.full.pdf+html.

18. Russell, T., *Commercial Advertising (RLE Advertising)* vol. 7, New York: Routledge, 2013.

19. Barabak, Mark Z., 'How Bill Clinton, Improbably, Became America's Favorite Politician', LATimes.com, 10 September 2014, http://www.latimes.com/nation/politics/politicsnow/la-pn-bill-clinton-americas-favorite-politician-20140910-story.html.

20. Sonner, M.W. and Wilcox, C., 'Forgiving and Forgetting: Public Support for Bill Clinton during the Lewinsky Scandal', *Political Science and Politics* 32:3, 1999, pp. 554–57.

21. 'What Made Bill Clinton Such a Popular President?', Quora, https://www.quora.com/What-made-Bill-Clinton-such-apopular-president#!n=12.

22. Hook, Janet, 'Poll: Bill Clinton Most Admired President of Past 25 years', *Washington Wire* (blog), *Wall Street Journal*, 15 June 2014, http://blogs.wsj.com/washwire/2014/06/15/poll-billclinton-most-admired-president-of-last-25-years.

23. Patel, Aakar, 'Everything You Need to Know about Narendra Modi', Livemint, 29 September 2011, http://www.livemint. com/

Opinion/5XGaq7Z1kVl7iSoHQhrVxN/Everythingyou-
need-to-know-about-Narendra-Modi.html.

24. Pathak, Anil, 'Modi's Meteoric Rise', *Times of India*,
Ahmedabad edition, 2 October 2001, http://timesofindia.
indiatimes.com/city/ahmedabad/Modis-meteoric rise/
articleshow/1459210533.cms.

25. Venkatesan, V., 'A Pracharak as Chief Minister', *Frontline*,
13 October 2001, http://www.frontline.in/static/html/
fl1821/18210310.htm.

26. Mehta, Harit, 'Six-Year Banishment Led to Narendra Modi's
Metamorphosis', *Times of India*, 1 April 2014, http://timesofindia.
indiatimes.com/news/Six-year-banishment-ledto-Narendra-
Modis-metamorphosis/articleshow/33040649.cms.

27. Bunsha, Dionne., 'A New Oarsman', *Frontline*, 13 October 2001,
http://www.frontline.in/static/html/fl1821/18210300.htm.

28. Pandey, Anurag, 'Arvind Kejriwal Biography—Rare Facts to
Know', LetUsPublish.com, 16 August 2014, http://www.
letuspublish.com/arvind-kejriwal-biography-rare-facts-know.

29. Makkar, Sahil, 'The Different Shades of Arvind Kejriwal',
Livemint, 26 November 2012, http://www.livemint.
com/Politics/XERu7Qq6eidzuQrpQewQcN/The-
differentshades-of-Arvind-Kejriwal.html.

30. Pradhan, Kunal and Vij-Aurora, Bhavna, 'An Uncommon Life',
IndiaToday.in, 27 December 2013, http://indiatoday.intoday.
in/story/newsmaker-2013-arvind-kejriwal-aam-aadmi-
partyiit-graduate/1/333235.html.

31. Bacani Jr, Cesar R., 'Arvind Kejriwal Biography', Ramon
Magsaysay Award Foundation, 13 February 2015, http://
www.rmaf.org.ph/newrmaf/main/awardees/awardee/
biography/141.

32. Verma, Jyoti, 'Of Rights and Wrongs', 6 August 2006, https://
right2information.wordpress.com/category/parivartan/page/2.

33. PTI, 'Anna Hazare Tells Arvind Kejriwal Not to Use His Name,
Photo for Votes as They Part Ways', *India Today*, 19 September
2012.

34. 'Assembly Elections December 2013 Results', Election Commission of India, 12 December 2013, http://eci.nic.in/eci_main/StatisticalReports/AE2013/CG   AE_2013_stat_report.pdf.

35. http://www.aamaadmiparty.org, 10 March 2015.

36. Express News Service, 'Arvind Kejriwal Express: Just 48 days in Power, but Every Day on the Front Page', *Indian Express*, 15 February 2014, http://indianexpress.com/article/india/politics/arvind-kejriwal-express-aam-aadmi-party-delhi-government/.

Chapter 3: Image Management: Theory and Practice

1. Cassidy, Anne, 'Political Brands: Who Gets Your Vote?', Theguardian.com, 2 April 2015, http://www.theguardian.com/media-network/2015/apr/02/politicalbrands-who-gets-your-vote.

2. Ibid.

3. Bennett, Bo., 'Hypothesis Contrary to Fact', LogicallyFallacious.com, 15 March 2015, http://www.logicallyfallacious.com/index.php/logical-fallacies/107-hypothesis-contrary-tofact.

4. Tetlock, Philip E. and Belkin, Aaron, eds., *Counterfactual Thought Experiments in World Politics: Logical, Methodological, and Psychological Perspectives*, New Jersey, NJ: Princeton University Press, 1996, http://aaronbelkin.org/pdfs/Counterfactual%20Thought%20Experiments%20in%20World%20Politics%20-%201st%20chpt.pdf .

5. 'Counterfactual Conditional', Wikipedia, 9 March 2015, http://en.wikipedia.org/wiki/Counterfactual_conditional.

6. Markman, KD, Gavanski, I, Sherman, SJ, McMullen, MN, 'The mental simulation of better and worse possible worlds', *Journal of Experimental Social Psychology*, 1993, pp. 87–109.

7. 'Three reasons to distrust "coulda, woulda, shoulda" thinking', http://www.csus.edu/indiv/m/merlinos/counterfactuals.html.

8. Miller, D.T. and Turnbull, W., 'The Counterfactual Fallacy: Confusing What Might Have Been with What Ought to Have Been', *Social Justice Research* 4:1, 1990, pp. 1–19.

9. 'Three reasons to distrust "coulda, woulda, shoulda" thinking', http://www.csus.edu/indiv/m/merlinos/counterfactuals.html.

10. Ibid.

11. Roese, Neal, 'Counterfactual Thinking', *Psychological Bulletin* vol. 121:1, 1997, pp. 133-148, http://www2.psych.ubc.ca/~schaller/Psyc590Readings/Roese1997.pdf.

12. Turner, M., 'Language and Literature', *SAGE Publications* vol. 15:1, 2006, pp. 17–27, http://lal.sagepub.com.

13. Byrne, *The Rational Imagination*.

14. Fearon, 'Counterfactuals and Hypothesis Testing in Political Science', *World Politics* vol.43:2, Cambridge University Press, 1991.

15. Ibid, pp. 169–195.

16. 'What is partial correlation', 3 August 2016, http://www.psychwiki.com/wiki/What_is_a_partial_correlation%3F.

17. PTI, 'Narendra Modi conspired to instigate Hindus post Godhra: Zakia Jafri's lawyer', *India Today*, 29 June 2013, http://indiatoday.intoday.in/story/narendra-modi-conspired-to-instigate hindus-postgodhra-zakia-jafri-lawyer/1/285967.html.

18. Ram, N., 'Narendra Modi and Why 2002 Cannot Go Away', *The Hindu*, 6 November 2013, http://www.thehindu.com/todays-paper/tp-opinion/narendra-modi-and-why-2002-cannot-go-away/article5318984.ece.

19. Ram, N., 'Narendra Modi and Why 2002 Cannot Go Away', *The Hindu*, 6 November 2013, http://www.thehindu.com/todayspaper/tp-opinion/narendra-modi-and-why-2002-cannot-goaway/article5318984.ece.

20. Majumder, Sanjoy, 'Narendra Modi "allowed" Gujarat 2002 anti-Muslim riots', BBC News, 22 April 2011, http://www.bbc.com/news/world-south-asia-13170914.

21. 'Gujarat Riot Death Toll Revealed', BBC News, 11 May 2005, http://news.bbc.co.uk/2/hi/south_asia/4536199.stm.

22. 'Harvest of Hatred', *The Hindu*, 16 December 2002, http://www. thehindu. com/2002/12/16/stories/2002121600531000.htm.

23. 'Harvest of Hatred', *The Hindu*, 16 December 2002, http://www. thehindu. com/2002/12/16/stories/2002121600531000.htm.

24. 'Gujarat result "harvest of hatred"', BBC News, 16 December 2002, http://news.bbc.co.uk/2/hi/south_asia/2580369.stm.

25. Khare, H., 'The Guilty Men of Ahemdabad', *The Hindu*, 7 March 2002, http://www. thehindu. com/2002/03/07/ stories/2002030700071000.htm.

26. 'Narendra Modi as Super Scapegoat', *The Hindu Editorials*, 31 May 2004, http://www.thehindu.com/2004/05/31/ stories/2004053101591000.htm.

27. Ilaiah, K., 'The Rise of Modi', *The Hindu*, 26 December 2002, http://www. thehindu.com/2002/12/26/stories/ 2002122600461000.htm.

28. Smith, Amy E.,'Local Connections: Electoral Institutions, Social Networks and Local Politicians in a Developing Democracy', 2011, http://opensiuc.lib.siu.edu/pnconfs_2011/13.

29. 'What MB Shah Commission Says about Modi', *Indian Express*, 10 March 2015, http://indianexpress.com/tag/m-b-shah- commission/.

30. Ghosh, Shamik,'Shah Panel Gives Clean Chit to Narendra Modi's govt in Land Allotment Cases, NDTV.com, 3 October 2012, http://www.ndtv.com/india-news/shah-panel-gives-clean- chit-to-narendra-modis-govt-in-land-allotment-cases-500873.

31. Mahurkar, Uday, 'CBI Chargesheet against Shah a Blow to Narendra Modi', IndiaToday.in, 5 September 2012, http:// indiatoday.intoday.in/story/cbi-chargesheet-against-amitshah- a-blow-to-narendra-modi/1/216153.html.

32. Manoj, C.L., 'Snoopgate Probe against Narendra Modi', *Economic Times*, 30 April 2014, http://articles.economictimes. indiatimes.com/2014-04-30/news/49523366_1_snoopgate- gulail-sitting-judge.

33. Press Information Bureau, Government of India, 26 December 2013, http://pib.nic.in/newsite/mbErel.aspx?relid=102144.

34. Ghosh, Deepshikha, 'Snoopgate: "Thankful" for Surveillance, Woman Tells Supreme Court', NDTV, 6 May 2014, http://www. ndtv.com/elections/article/election-2014/snoopgatethankful-for-surveillance-woman-tells-supreme-court-519233.

35. Rao, Raghvendra, 'Narendra Modi's Selfie-Goal: FIRs Filed for "flouting" Poll Code', *Indian Express*, 1 May 2014, http://indianexpress.com/article/india/politics/ec-orders-actionagainst-modi-for-political-speech-after-casting-his-vote.

36. Rao, Raghvendra, 'Narendra Modi's Selfie-Goal: FIRs Filed for "flouting" Poll Code', *Indian Express*, 1 May 2014, http://indianexpress.com/article/india/politics/ec-orders-actionagainst-modi-for-political-speech-after-casting-his-vote.

37. Srivastava, Pallavi, 'Why Arvind Kejriwal Is the Tata Nano Of Indian Politics', *Business Insider India*, 11 June 2014, http:// www.businessinsider.in/Why-ArvindKejriwal-Is-The-Tata-Nano-Of-Indian Politics/articleshow/36397276.cms.

38. 'If you want to be an anarchist, go join Naxals: Modi raps Kejriwal in Delhi', Firstpost.com, 10 January 2015, http://www. firstpost.com/politics/if-you-want-to-be-an-anarchist-go-join-naxals-modiraps-kejriwal-in-delhi-2039671.html.

39. 'Kejriwal is a Liar', ABP Live, 5 February 2015, http://www. abplive.in/india-news/kejriwal-is-a-liarkiran-bedi-150647.

40. 'BJP's Nupur Sharma Compares Kejriwal to a Monkey', *DNA*, 24 January 2015, http://www.dnaindia.com/india/report-bjp-s-nupur-sharma-compares-kejriwal-toa-monkey-2055470.

41. Datta, Saikat, 'The People Legislate', *Outlook*, 25 April 2011, http:// www.outlookindia.com/article/the-peoplelegislate/271401.

42. Parashar, Arpit, 'The Ten Men on the Lokpal Bill Drafting Committee', *Tehelka*, 9 April 2011, http://archive.tehelka.com/ story_main49.asp?filename=Ws090411TheTenMen.asp.

43. Raman, Anuradha, 'The After Math', *Outlook*, 12 September 2011.

44. Menon, Sreelatha, 'Claims That Hazare's Movement is US Funded Baseless: Arvind', *Business Standard*, 31 August 2011, http://www.business-standard.com/article/economy-

policy/claims-that-hazare-s-movement-is-us-funded-baselessarvind-111083100109_1.html.

45. Raman, Anuradha, 'Anna, the Maskot', *Outlook*, 11 June 2012, http://www.outlookindia.com/article/anna-themaskot/281093.

46. French, A., Smith, G., 'Measuring Political Brand Equity: A Consumer Oriented Approach', *European Journal of Marketing*, 44 (3-4), 2010, pp. 460-467, https://dspace.lboro.ac.uk/dspace-jspui/bitstream/2134/14793/3/Political%20Brand%20Equity%20(Last%20Version).pdf.

47. Allen, D.E. and Olson, J., 'Conceptualizing and Creating Brand Personality: A Narrative Theory Approach', *Advances in Consumer Research* 22, 1995, pp. 392.

48. Aaker, J.L., 'Dimensions of Brand Personality', *Journal of Marketing Research* 34, August 1997, pp. 347.

49. Smith, G., 'Conceptualizing and Testing Brand Personality in British Politics', *Journal of Political Marketing* 8:3, 2009, pp.209–32.

50. Pande, Shamni, 'Just the Right Image', *Business Today*, 8 June 2014, http://www.businesstoday.in/magazine/case-study/case-study-strategy-tactics-behind-creation-of-brandnarendra-modi/story/206321.html.

51. Eisenbach, D., Fynt, L., *One Nation Under Sex: How the Private Lives of Presidents, First Ladies and Their Lovers Changed Course of History*, New York: Palgrave Macmillan, 2011.

52. Jones, M., 'Monica Lewinsky–Bill Clinton Scandal: 7 Things We Learned from PBS Documentary "Clinton"', IBTimes.com, 16 February 2012, http://www.ibtimes.com/monica-lewinsky-bill-clinton-scandal-7-things-we-learned-pbs-documentary-clinton-411708.

53. Jones, M., 'Monica Lewinsky-Bill Clinton Scandal: 7 Things We Learned From PBS Documentary "Clinton"', IBTimes.com, 16 February 2012, http://www.ibtimes.com/monica-lewinsky-bill-clinton-scandal-7-things-we-learned-pbs-documentary-clinton-411708.

54. Ibid.

55. 'On This Day: President Clinton Admits Affair with Monica Lewisnky', FindingDulcinea.com, 17 August 2011, http://www.findingdulcinea.com/news/on-this-day/July-August-08/Onthis-Day--President-Clinton-Admits-Affair.html.

56. Elks, Jennifer, 'Coca-Cola Gives Back, Helps the World Live Positively', SustainableBrands.com, 1 October 2012, http://www.sustainablebrands.com/news_and_views/blog/cocacola-gives-back-helps-world-live-positively.

57. Pande, S., 'The Strategy and Tactics Behind the Creation of Brand Modi', India Today Group, 19 May 2014, https://in.finance.yahoo.com/news/strategy-tactics-behind-creation-brand-053541220.html.

58. Ibid.

59. Ibid.

60. Ibid.

61. Ibid.

62. PTI, 'AAP MLAs Choose Arvind Kejriwal as Leader in Delhi Assembly', *Economic Times*, 9 December 2013, http://articles.economictimes.indiatimes.com/2013-12-09/news/44989260_1_arvind-kejriwal-aam-aadmi-party-seniorparty-leader.

63. Ghosh, Shamik, 'Arvind Kejriwal Calls Off Sit-In That Gridlocked Delhi, Shocked Centre', NDTV, 22 January 2014, http://www.ndtv.com/delhi-news/arvind-kejriwal-calls-offsit-in-that-gridlocked-delhi-shocked-centre-548482.

64. PTI, 'AAP Prepares for Fresh Elections', *Times of India*, 21 May 2014, http://timesofindia.indiatimes.com/city/delhi/AAPprepares-for-fresh-polls-in-Delhi-Kejriwal-apologizes-forquitting-midway/articleshow/35418704.cms.

65. Coombs, W.T., 'Protecting Organization Reputation during Crisis: The Development and Application of Situational Crisis Communication Theory', *Corporate Reputation Review* 10, 2007, pp. 163–76.

66. Benoit, William L., 'Image Repair Discourse and Crisis Communication', *Public Relations Review* 23:2, 1997, http://

embanet.vo.llnwd.net/o18/USC/CMGT 502/Week11/docs/
CMGT 502_w11_ImageRepair.pdf

67. Ibid, pp. 177–86.

68. Aaker, D.A., *Building Strong Brands*, Simon and Schuster, 2012, http://books.simonandschuster.com/Building-Strong-Brands/David-A-Aaker/9781451674750.

69. Pande, S, 'Just the Right Image', *Business Today*, 8 June 2014, http://www.businesstoday.in/magazine/case-study/casestudy-strategy-tactics-behind-creation-of-brand-narendramodi/story/206321.html.

70. Moorthi, Y.L.R., *Brand Management*, Uttar Pradesh: Vikas Publishing House Pvt. Ltd, 2009.

71. 'About Zulfiqar Ali Bhutto', Bhutto.org, http://www.bhutto.org/about-bhutto.php.

72. Syed, Anwar H., 'ZA Bhutto's Self-Characterizations and Pakistani Political Culture', *Asian Survey* 18:12, 1978, pp.1250–66.

73. Pande, S, 'The Strategy and Tactics Behind the Creation of Brand Modi', India Today Group, 19 May 2014, https://in.finance.yahoo.com/news/strategy-tactics-behind-creation-brand-053541220.html.

74. Benoit, W.L, 'Image Repair Discourse and Crisis Communication', *Public Relations Review* vol.23, 1997, pp. 177.

75. Augustine, N.R., 'Managing the Crisis you Tried to Prevent', November-December 1995, https://hbr.org/1995/11/managing-the-crisis-you-tried-to-prevent.

76. Kaplan, Tamara, 'The Tylenol Crisis: How Effective Public Relations Saved Johnson & Johnson', Aerobiologicalengineering.com, 28 September 2015, http://www.aerobiologicalengineering.com/wxk116/TylenolMurders/crisis.html.

77. Based on extrapolating from research project developed by Dheeraj Sharma with doctoral student Varsha Verma.

78. 'Full Text: Prime Minister Narendra Modi's speech on 68th Independence Day', *Indian Express*, 16 August 2014, http://indianexpress.com/article/india/india-others/full-text-prime-minister-narendra-modis-speech-on-68th-independence-day/.

79. Nongrum, Dianne, 'Full Text: Rahul Gandhi's fierce attack on Modi govt in Lok Sabha', *India Today*, 2 March 2016, http://indiatoday.intoday.in/story/full-text-rahul-gandhis-fierce-attack-on-modi-govt-in-lok-sabha/1/610490.html.

80. 'Prime Minister Narendra Modi's Speech at British Parliament: Full Text', NDTV.com, 13 November 2015, http://www.ndtv.com/india-news/prime-minister-narendra-modis-address-at-british-parliament-full-speech-1242831.

81. 'Full Text of Prime Minister Narendra Modi's Speech at the India-China Business Forum in Shanghai', NDTV.com, 16 May 2015, http://www.ndtv.com/india-news/full-text-of-prime-minister-narendra-modis-speech-at-the-india-china-business-forum-in-shanghai-763508.

82. 'Read full text of Arvind Kejriwal's first speech as Delhi CM', TNN, 14 February 2015, http://timesofindia.indiatimes.com/delhi-elections-2015/top-stories/Read-full-text-of-Arvind-Kejriwals-first-speech-as-Delhi-CM/articleshow/46247444.cms.

83. Maass, Anne and Salvi, Daniela, 'Language Use in Intergroup Contexts: The Linguistic Intergroup Bias', *Journal of Personality and Social Psychology* vol. 57:6, 1989, pp. 981-993, http://dspace.ubvu.vu.nl/bitstream/handle/1871/3882/8922.pdf?sequence=1.

Chapter 4: Managing Workforce

1. Roberts, Richard G., 'The Art of Apology: When and How to Seek Forgiveness', *Family Practice Management* 14:7, 2007, pp. 44–49.

2. Kerfoot, Karlene, 'The Art of Truth Telling: Handling Failure with Disclosure and Apology, Nursing Economics', 2006, pp. 29–30.

3. Express News Service, 'Arvind Kejriwal Apologises to Delhi for "Quitting Midway", Seeks Fresh Elections', *Indian Express*, 21 May 2014.

4. Pandey, Alok, "'Apologise to the People of Bihar," Nitish Kumar Tells Party Workers in Patna', NDTV, 1 March 2015, http://www.ndtv.com/india-news/apologise-to-the-people-of-biharnitish-kumar-asks-party-workers-in-patna-743446.

5. PTI, 'Hang me if I have committed any crime, but no apology, Narendra Modi says', *Times of India*, 16 April 2014, http://timesofindia.indiatimes.com/news/Hang-me-if-I-have-committed-any-crime-but-no-apology-Narendra-Modi-says/articleshow/33832367.cms.

6. Roberts, R., 'Art of Apology', http://www.aafp.org/fpm/2007/0700/p44.html#sec-2

7. Bhattacharya, D.P., 'Sadbhavana Mission II: Narendra Modi Meets Businessmen from Muslim Community, Talks Development', *Economic Times*, 8 February 2014, http://articles.economictimes.indiatimes.com/2014-02-08/news/47148778_1_muslim-youth-narendra-modi-muslimcommunity.

8. PTI, 'In message to Muslims, Narendra Modi says 'Will Reach Out To All''', *DNA*, 23 April 2014, http:// http://www.ndtv.com/elections-news/in-message-tomuslims-narendra-modi-says-will-reach-out-to-all-558423.

9. Gurumurthy, S., 'Modi's Symbolism and Secularism', *New Indian Express*, 20 May 2014, http://www.newindianexpress.com/columns/Modis-Symbolism-and-Secularism/2014/05/20/article2233789.ece.

10. Dutta, Anirudha, 'Why Can't I Refuse a Skull Cap and Still Be Secular?', Firstpost.com, 21 November 2011, http://www.firstpost.com/blogs/%E2%80%9Cwhy-can%E2%80%99t-irefuse-a-skull-cap-and-still-be-secular%E2%80%9D-136313.html.

11. Colvin, Ross and Bhattacharjya, Satarupa, 'I'm a Hindu Nationalist, Patriotic: Narendra Modi', *Hindustan Times*, 27 July 2013, http://www.hindustantimes.com/allaboutnarendramodi/i-m-a-hindu-nationalist-patrioticnarendra-modi/article1-1091198.aspx.

12. 'Women and Child Development Projects and Initiatives', Gujarat State Portal, http://www.gujaratindia.com/initiatives/initiatives.htm.

13. Agarwal, Vibhuti, 'India's Politicians Trash-Talk Their Rivals', *India Real Time* (blog), *Wall Street Journal*, 29 April 2014, http://blogs.wsj.com/indiarealtime/2014/04/29/indiaspoliticians-trash-talk-their-rivals.

14. 'Narendra Modi Elected BJP Parliamentary Leader, Thanks Advani and Vajpayee', IndiaToday.in, 20 May 2014, http://indiatoday.intoday.in/story/narendra-modi-pm-bjpparliamentary-party-leader-rajnath-singh/1/362693.html.

15. Chauhan, Chetan, 'Modi's Govt Puts in Place Appraisal System for Ministers', *Hindustan Times*, 2 June 2014, http://www.hindustantimes.com/india-news/govt-puts-in-place-appraisalsystem-for-ministers/article1-1225380.aspx.

16. Lim, Thomas, 'Modi Bowing at the Steps of Parliament, Emotional Speech Moves Nation', *Meghalaya Times*, 5 March 2015, http://www.meghalayatimes.info/index.php/editorial/25245-modi-bowing-at-the-steps-of-parliamentemotional-speech-moves-nation.

17. Malik, Surabhi, 'From Narendra Modi's Team, Some Stats: 437 Rallies, 5827 Events, 3 Lakh Kilometres', NDTV, 9 May 2014, http://www.ndtv.com/elections/article/election-2014/fromnarendra-modi-s-team-some-stats-437-rallies-5827-events-3-lakh-kilometres-521182.

18. Archibald, Joleen, 'Understanding and improving your own charisma', 9 September 2014, https://leadershiparchways.com/2014/09/09/understanding-and-improving-your-own-charisma.

19. Shamir, B., House, R.J. and Arthur, M.B., 'The Motivational Effects of Charismatic Leadership: A Self-Concept Based Theory', *Organization Science* 4:4, 1993, pp. 577–94.

20. Kamat, Swapnil, 'Narendra Modi's Skills in Presenting— Lessons to Learn', *Economic Times*, 26 June 2014, http://

articles.economictimes.indiatimes.com/2014-06-26/
news/50884927_1_body-language-audience-narendra-modi.

21. Kumar, Charulata Ravi, 'Speaking Like Modi', *Indian Express*,
    23 May 2014, http://indianexpress.com/article/opinion/
    columns/speaking-like-modi.

22. Riggio, Ronald E., 'What Is Charisma and Charismatic
    Leadership?', *Psychology Today*, 7 October 2012, https://
    www.psychologytoday.com/blog/cutting-edge-
    leadership/201210/what-is-charisma-and-charismatic-
    leadership.

23. Shamir, B., House, R. J., and Arthur, M. B., 'The Motivational
    Effects of Charismatic leadership: A Self-concept Based theory',
    Organization Science, 1993, pp. 577-594.

24. 'CM Narendra Modi advocates development on 3 S—Scale,
    Speed and Skill to realize India's century', 09 January 2012,
    http://www.narendramodi.in/cm-narendra-modi-advocates-
    development-on-3-s-%E2%80%93-scale-speed-and-skill-to-
    realize-india%E2%80%99s-century-2-4.

25. 'Full text of Budget 2015-16 speech', *The Hindu*, 28 February
    2015, http://www.thehindu.com/news/resources/full-text-of-
    budget-201516-speech/article6945026.ece.

26. PTI, 'In message to Muslims, Narendra Modi says "will reach
    out to all"', NDTV.com, 23 April 2014, http://www.ndtv.com/
    elections-news/in-message-to-muslims-narendra-modi-says-
    will-reach-out-to-all-558423.

27. PTI, 'Focus on "skill, scale and speed" to compete with China:
    PM', *The Hindu*, 8 June 2014, http://www.thehindu.com/
    news/national/focus-on-skill-scale-and-speed-to-compete-
    with-china-pm/article6094934.ece.

28. Dasgupta, Piyasree, 'Modi Wave: The Men behind India's
    Biggest Brand Story', Firstpost.com, 11 June 2014, http://www.
    firstpost.com/politics/modi-wave-the-men-behind-indias-
    biggest-brand-story-1563957.html.

29. Raja, Aditi, 'Statue of Unity Project Rusts, No New Iron in
    2 months', *Indian Express*, 25 June 2014, http://indianexpress.

com/article/india/india-others/statue-of-unity-project-rusts-no-new-iron-in-2-months/.

30. PTI, 'Modi Will Never Be PM, but He Can Sell Tea: Mani Shankar Aiyar', Firstpost.com, 18 January 2014, http://www.firstpost.com/politics/modi-will-never-be-pm-but-he-can-selltea-mani-shankar-aiyar-1345419.html.

31. 'Round Two of "Chai Pe Charcha" Will Focus on Women Empowerment', 4 March 2014, http://www.narendramodi.in/round-two-of-chai-pe-charcha-will-focus-on-womenempowerment.

32. 'Narendra Modi's Chai Pe Charcha: How Global Media Covered It', IndiaToday.in, 14 February 2014, http://indiatoday.intoday.in/story/narendra-modis-chai-pe-charchaevent-gets-rave-reviews-in-global-media/1/343440.html; PTI, 'Modi Connects with the People through His "Chai Pe Charcha" Campaign', *Times of India*, 12 February 2014, http://timesofindia.indiatimes.com/india/Modi-connectswith-the-people-through-his-chai-pe-charcha-campaign/articleshow/30292508.cms.

33. 'Agenda Setting Theory', University of Twente, http://www.utwente.nl/cw/theorieenoverzicht/Theory%20Clusters/Mass%20Media/Agenda-Setting_Theory.

34. 'Narendra Modi's Electoral Milestone: 437 Rallies, 3 Lakh Km', *Times of India*, 30 April 2014, http://timesofindia.indiatimes.com/news/Narendra-Modis-electoral-milestone-437-rallies-3-lakh-km/articleshow/34400255.cms.

35. Mission Protect India, https://www.youtube.com/watch?v=Nt-CwQuv7ik.

36. Dosanjh, Ujjal, 'Amitabh Bachchan hosting the Modi victory bash—a blunder', *Indian Express*, 26 May 2016, http://indianexpress.com/article/blogs/amitabh-bachchan-hosting-the-modi-victory-bash-a-blunder-two-year-narendra-modi-govt-anniversary-2820251/.

37. http://planningcommission.nic.in/plans/stateplan/Presentations12_13/gujrat_1213.pdf.

38. http://planningcommission.nic.in/plans/stateplan/
    Presentations12_13/gujrat_1213.pdf.

Chapter 5: Effective Media Usage

1. Maass, A., Milesi, A., Zabbini, S. and Stahlberg, D., 'Linguistic
    Intergroup Bias: Differential Expectancies or In-Group
    Protection?', *Journal of Personality and Social Psychology* 68:1,
    1995, pp. 116.
2. Douglas, K.M. and Sutton, R.M., 'Effects of Communication
    Goals and Expectancies on Language Abstraction', *Journal of
    Personality and Social Psychology* 84:4, 2003, pp. 682.
3. Greenstein, Fred I., *The Presidential Difference: Leadership Style
    from FDR to Barack Obama*, third ed., Princeton, NJ: Princeton
    University Press, 2009.
4. 'India Has Way Too Many Things Named after Nehru–
    Gandhi Family', NewsEastWest.com, 30 May 2014, http://
    newseastwest.com/india-has-way-too-many-things-
    namedafter-nehru-gandhi-family.
5. '10 Slogans That Define India's Political History', IndiaToday.
    in, 12 March 2015, http://indiatoday.intoday.in/gallery/
    mass-appeal-slogans-bjp-congress-indira-gandhi-atalbihari-
    vajpayee/7/9334.html.
6. 'Richard Nixon: Impact and Legacy', Miller Center of Public
    Affairs, University of Virginia, 3 March 2016, http://
    millercenter.org/president/biography/nixon-impact-andlegacy.
7. Rauch, Jonathan, 'What Nixon Wrought: The Worst
    Presidency of the Century', JonathanRauch.com, 16 May 1994,
    http://www. jonathanrauch.com/jrauch_articles/nixon_20th_
    centurys_worst_president.
8. Grossman, L.K., *Electronic Republic: Reshaping American
    Democracy for the Information Age*, New York: Viking Books, 1995.
9. O'Day, J. Brian, *Political Campaign Planning Manual, A Step by
    Step Guide to Winning Elections*, National Democratic Institute,
    Washington DC, 1 January 2003, https://www.ndi.org/
    node/13124.

10. O'Day, J. Brian, *Political Campaign Planning Manual, A Step by Step Guide to Winning Elections*, National Democratic Institute, Washington DC, 1 January 2003, https://www.ndi.org/node/13124.

11. 'Mission Vistaar', AamAadmiParty.org, 30 June 2014, http://www.aamaadmiparty.org/mission-vistaar.

12. Ghose, D. and Vatsa, A., 'The Big Picture: What's AAP', *Indian Express*, 15 February 2015, http://indianexpress.com/article/india/indiaothers/whats-aap/.

13. Ibid.

14. Ibid.

15. 'AAP's Blueprint for Delhi', AamAadmiParty.org, 08 January 2015, http://www.aamaadmiparty.org/manifesto-2015.

16. Ghose, Dipankar and Vatsa, Aditi, 'The Big Picture: What's AAP', *Indian Express*, 15 February 2015, http://indianexpress.com/article/india/india-others/whats-aap.

17. Levitt, T., 'Marketing Myopia', *Harvard Business Review* 38:4, 1960, pp. 24–47.

18. Kohli, A.K., Jaworski, B.J. and Kumar, A., 'MARKOR: A Measure of Market Orientation', *Journal of Marketing Research* 30:4, 1993, pp. 467–77.

19. Verma, Harsh, 'Burhan Wani, Protests, Brand Identification and Battle of Ideas', *Marketing Crow* (blog), 11 February 2015, https://marketingcrow.wordpress.com. https://marketingcrow.wordpress.com/.

Chapter 6: Digital Media Campaigning

1. Leppäniemi, M., Karjaluoto, H., Lehto, H. and Goman, A., 'Targeting Young Voters in a Political Campaign: Empirical Insights into an Interactive Digital Marketing Campaign in the 2007 Finnish General Election', *Journal of Nonprofit & Public Sector Marketing* 22:1, 2010, pp. 14–37.

2. Bakker, T.P. and de Vreese, C.H., 'Good News for the Future? Young People, Internet Use, and Political Participation', *Communication Research* 38: 4, 2011, pp. 451–70.

3. 'Narendra Modi Embraces Musion's Hologram Technology
    Once More in Bid to Lead India', Musion.com, http://musion.
    com/?portfolio=narendra-modi-campaign-2014.

4. Vij, Bhavna, Aurora, B., 'Lok Sabha Elections 2014: Meet the
    Backroom Boys at the Forefront of Narendra Modi's Victory',
    Economic Times, 18 May 2014, http://articles.economictimes.
    indiatimes.com/2014-05-18/news/49926059_1_
    narendramodi-modiji-rss.

5. 'Vision of Modi', BJP.org, 10 March 2015, http://www.bjp.org/
    en/core-issues/vision-of-modi.

6. http://www.cag.gov.in/study-reports.

7. Jain, Pankaj, 'AAP Launches Delhi Dialogue Ahead of Polls',
    IndiaToday.in, 12 November 2014, http://indiatoday.intoday.in/
    story/aap-delhi-dialogue-delhi-assemblyelections/1/400438.
    html.

8. Alexandrova, Ekaterina, 'Using New Media Effectively: An
    Analysis of Barack Obama's Election Campaign Aimed at Young
    Americans', Fordham University, New York, 2010, http://www.
    academia.edu/1526998/Using_New_Media_Effectively_an_
    Analysis_of_Barack_Obamas_Election_Campaign_Aimed_
    at_Young_Americans.

9. 'Obama Dominating Highly-Charged Youth Vote in Presidential
    Race, Harvard Poll Finds', IOP.Harvard.edu, 24 April
    2008, http://www.iop.harvard.edu/april-24-2008-obama-
    dominating-highly-charged-youth-vote-presidentialrace-
    harvard-poll-finds.

10. 'Ganz, M., 'Organizing Obama: Campaign, Organizing,
    Movement', (unpublished), American Sociological Association
    Annual Meeting, San Francisco, August 2009.

11. Alexandrova, 'Using New Media Effectively', http://www.
    academia.edu/1526998/Using_New_Media_Effectively_an_
    Analysis_of_Barack_Obamas_Election_Campaign_Aimed_
    at_Young_Americans.

12. Stracabosko, Nika, 'Metacoverage of US Presidential Elections
    1988, 2008, 2012', MakingScienceNews.com, 1 June 2014,

http://www.makingsciencenews.com/catalogue/papers/712/view.

13. Hjarvard, S., 'The Mediatization of Society: A Theory of the Media as Agents of Social and Cultural Change', *Nordicom Review*, 2008, pp.106.

14. Stracabosko, N., 'Metacoverage of US Presidential Elections 1988, 2008, 2012', MakingScienceNews.com, 1 June 2014, www.makingsciencenews.com/catalogue/papers/712/download.

15. Stracabosko,N., 'Metacoverage of US Presidential Elections 1988, 2008, 2012'; Kerbel, M.R., *Remote and Controlled: Media Politics in a Cynical Age*, Boulder, CO: Westview, 1999.

16. Krotz, F., *Mediatisierung: Fallstudien zum Wandel von Kommunikation*, Wiesbaden: VS Verlag für Sozialwissenschaften, 2007.

17. Schillemans, T., *Mediatization and Public Services: How Organizations Adapt to News Media*, Frankfurt: Peter Lang, 2012.

18. Krotz, F., *Mediatisierung: Fallstudien zum Wandel von Kommunikation*, Wiesbaden: VS Verlag für Sozialwissenschaften, 2007.

19. Donges, P., 'Politische Kommunikation in der Schweiz. Medialisierung eines "Sonderfalls"?', *PolitischeKommunikation in der Schweiz*, ed. P. Donges, Berne: Haupt, 2005, pp. 7–26.

20. Strömbäck, J., 'Four Phases of Mediatization: An Analysis of the Mediatization of Politics', *International Journal of Press/Politics* vol. 13, 2008, pp. 228–246, http://hij.sagepub.com/content/13/3/228.abstract.

21. Altheide, D.L., 'Media Logic and Political Communication', *Political Communication*, California: Sage Publications, 2008.

22. Kriesi, H., Lavenex, S., Esser, F.,Matthes, J., Bühlmann, M., Bochsler, D., 'Mediatization as a Challenge: Media Logic versus Political Logic', *Democracy in the Age of Globalization and Mediatization*, Basingstoke: Palgrave Macmillan, 2013, pp. 155–76.

23. Altheide, D. L., Snow R. P., *Media Worlds in the Post Journalism Era*, Transaction Publishers, 1991.

24. Plasser, Frank, Plasser, Gunda, *Global Political Campaigning: A Worldwide Analysis of Campaign Professionals and Their Practices*, West Port: Praeger, 2002.

25. Thapa, Rekhi, 'Barack Obama's Use of the New Media in His Election Campaign', Prezi.com, 22 September 2014, https://prezi.com/xbpyern4vb2q/barack-obamas-use-of-the-newmedia-in-his-election-campaign.

26. 'Narendra Modi Is Fourth-Most Followed Twitter World Leader, Finds New Twiplomacy Report', Firstpost.com, 25 June 2014, http://tech.firstpost.com/news-analysis/narendra-modi-fourth-followed-twitter-world-leader-findsnew-twiplomacy-report-226415.html.

27. PTI, 'Modi wishes best of health to Sonia Gandhi', *DNA*, 27 August 2013, http://www.dnaindia.com/india/report-narendra-modi-wishes-best-of-health-to-sonia-gandhi-1880552,27.

28. 'Mission 272+: How the BJP used the Internet to power its campaign', Rediff.com, 25 April 2014, http://www.rediff.com/news/interview/ls-election-mission-272-how-the-bjp-used-the-internet-to-power-its-campaign/20140425.htm.

29. Ghosh, Mohul, 'Narendra Modi vs Arvind Kejriwal—Who Won the Campaign War', Track.in, 30 May 2014, http://trak.in/tags/business/2014/05/13/narendra-modi-arvind-kejriwalcampaign-war.

30. Nair, D., 'How IITians Helped Engineer AAP's win', Rediff.com, 11 February 2015, http://www.rediff.com/news/report/delhipolls-how-iitians-helped-engineer-aaps-win/20150211.htm.

31. Harihar, Apeksha, 'Social Media Strategy Review: Aam Aadmi Party', Socialsamosa.com, 13 March 2014, http://www.socialsamosa.com/2014/03/social-media-strategy-reviewaam-aadmi-party.

32. Ibid.

33. Chowdhury, Arghya Roy, 'Decoded: Kejriwal's Strategy to Become the Top Leader of Anti-NaMo Brigade', *DNA*, 20 January

2016, http://www.dnaindia.com/india/report-arvindkejriwal-and-the-art-of-staying-in-news-2167692.

34. Harihar, 'Social Media Strategy Review'.

35. 'Social Media Strategy Review: Aam Aadmi Party', Socialsamosa.com, 13 March 2014, http://www.socialsamosa.com/2014/03/social-media-strategy-review-aam-aadmi-party/.

36. Ibid.

37. Ibid.

38. 'Using New Media Effectively: An Analysis of Barack Obama's Election Campaign Aimed at Young Americans', Fordham University, http://www.academia.edu/1526998/Using_New_Media_Effectively_an_Analysis_of_Barack_Obamas_Election_Campaign_Aimed_at_Young_Americans.

39. Stample, Laura, 'Obama Spent More On Online Ads Than It Cost To Build The Lincoln Memorial', *Business Insider*, 5 November 2012, http://www.businessinsider.com/infographic-obamaromney-final-ad-spend-2012-11.

40. Christensen, Jen, 'Obama Outspends Romney on Online Ads', CNN Politics, 4 June 2012, http://edition.cnn.com/2012/06/03/politics/online-campaign-spending.

41. Rice, Alexis, 'Campaigns Online: The Profound Impact of the Internet, Blogs, and E-Technologies in Presidential Political Campaigning', Center for the Study of American Government at Johns Hopkins University, January 2004, http://www.campaignsonline.org/reports/online.pdf.

42. Ibid.

43. Organizing for Action, https://www.barackobama.com/about-ofa/.

44. Stelter, Brian, 'Enticing Text Messagers in a Get-Out-the-Vote Push', *New York Times*, 2008, http://www.nytimes.com/2008/08/18/us/politics/18message.html.

45. Heffernan, Virginia, 'The YouTube Presidency', *New York Times Magazine*, 10 April 2009, http://www.nytimes.com/2009/04/12/magazine/12wwlnmedium-t.html.

46. 'Use of New Media Effectively: Analysis of Barack Obama's Election Campaign Aimed at Young Americans', Fordham

University, http://www.academia.edu/1526998/Using_
New_Media_Effectively_an_Analysis_of_Barack_Obamas_
Election_Campaign_Aimed_at_Young_Americans.

47. Gregory, Paul Roderick, 'Inside Putin's Campaign of Social
Media Trolling and Faked Ukrainian Crimes', *Forbes*, 11 May
2014, http://www.forbes.com/sites/paulroderickgregory/
2014/05/11/inside-putins-campaign-ofsocial-media-trolling-
and-faked-ukrainian-crimes.

48. Luhn, Alec, 'Pro-Kremlin journalists win medals for "objective"
coverage of Crimea', *Guardian*, 5 May 2014, https://www.
theguardian.com/world/2014/may/05/vladimir-putin-pro-
kremlin-journalists-medals-objective-crimea.

Chapter 7: Campaign Financing

1. Hofstadter, Richard, *The Age of Reform: From Bryan to F.D.R.*,
New York: Vintage, 1955.

2. Beyme, Klaus von, *Political Parties in Western Democracies*,
Aldershot, UK: Gower, 1985.

3. Scarrow, Susan E., 'Political Finance in Comparative Perspective',
Annual Review of Political Science 10, 23 January 2007, pp.193-210.

4. Scherer, Michael, 'Exclusive: Obama's 2012 Digital Fundraising
Outperformed 2008', Time.com, 15 November 2012, http://
swampland.time.com/2012/11/15/exclusive-obamas-2012-
digital-fundraising-outperformed-2008.

5. Moffatt, Zac, 'Successes of the Romney and Republican Digital
Efforts in 2012', TargetedVictory.com, 11 December 2012,
http://www.targetedvictory.com/2012/12/11/success-of-
theromney-republican-digital-efforts-2012.

6. Roller, E. and Stamm, S., '"Doomed": Why Do Fundraising
Emails Sound So Scary?', *National Journal*, 30 May 2014,
http://www.nationaljournal.com/s/65822/doomed-why-
dofundraising-emails-sound-so-scary.

7. Scherer, Michael, 'Exclusive: Obama's 2012 Digital Fundraising
Outperformed 2008', Time.com, 15 November 2012, http://

swampland.time.com/2012/11/15/exclusive-obamas-2012-digital-fundraising-outperformed-2008/.

8. Doherty, Brendan J., *The Rise of the President's Permanent Campaign*, Lawrence, KS: University Press of Kansas, 2012.

9. '6 Most Profitable Fundraising Dinners and Events', FinancesOnline.com, 15 March 2015, http://financesonline. com/6-most-profitable-fundraising-dinnersand-events.

10. IANS, 'AAP Raises More Than Rs 50 Lakh at Fundraising Event Organised by Traders' Wing', Firstpost.com, 1 December 2014, http://www.firstpost.com/politics/aap-raises-rs-50-lakh-fundraising-event-organised-traders-wing-1828857.html.

11. Kamat, Payal, 'The Obamafication of Indian Political Campaigns', *South Asia @ LSE* (blog), 17 March 2014, http:// blogs.lse.ac.uk/southasia/2014/03/17/the-obamafication-ofindian-political-campaigns.

12. Agencies, 'BJP Launches Special Fund Raising Campaigns in J-K', *Indian Express*, 1 July 2011, http://indianexpress. com/article/india/regional/bjp-launches-special-fund-raisingcampaign-in-jk.

Chapter 8: News Media Management

1. 'Exclusive: Read Full Interview of Narendra Modi to Rajat Sharma in Aap Ki Adalat (Part 2)', India TV, 13 June 2014, http://www.indiatvnews.com/politics/national/read-full-interview-of-narendra-modi-rajat-sharma-aap-kiadalat-16533.html.

2. Gheta, Irfan Iqbal, 'Narendra Modi Walks Away Victorious from "Aap Ki Adalat"', *DNA*, 13 April 2014, http://www. dnaindia.com/analysis/standpoint-narendra-modi-walksaway-victorious-from-aap-ki-adalat-1977932.

3. Jackson, John S., 'The Making of a Senator: Barack Obama and the 2004 Illinois Senate Race', *Paul Simon Public Policy Institute Review*, 2006, pp. 25, http://opensiuc.lib.siu.edu/cgi/viewcontent.cgi?article=1004&context=ppi_papers.

Chapter 9: Winning Election through Campaign Management

1. Parashar, Sudarshan, 'What Are the Main Reasons People Have for Supporting Congress?', Quora, 2 March 2013, http://www.quora.com/What-are-the-main-reasons-peoplehave-for-supporting-Congress.

2. Desai, Santosh, 'Vote for Rep, and Not Ruler, Who Can Bring Real Change', *Times of India*, 11 February 2015, http://timesofindia.indiatimes.com/elections/delhi-elections-2015/top-stories/Vote-for-rep-and-not-ruler-who-can-bring-realchange/articleshow/46194042.cms.

3. O'Day, J Brian, 'Political Campaign Planning Manual: A Step by Step Guide to Winning Elections', National Democratic Institute, 2009, https://www.ndi.org/files/Political_Campaign_Planning_Manual_Malaysia.pdf.

4. Issenberg, Sasha, 'How Obama's Team Used Big Data to Rally Voters', *MIT Technology Review*, 19 December 2012, http://www.technologyreview.com/featuredstory/509026/howobamas-team-used-big-data-to-rally-voters.

5. 'Our Vision', AamAadmiParty.org, 10 March 2015, http://www.aamaadmiparty.org/our-vision.

6. Survey conducted by Dheeraj Sharma (IIM–A) for the purpose of this study on two national and one regional party contestants with a sample size of 385, which comprised 210 male and 175 female residents of Delhi, via mall intercept method.

7. Mall-intercept survey: A survey method where the data collector collects responses in shopping malls across the region, by stopping people (intercepting) in public places. It is often considered an easy and cost-effective method of data collection.

8. Survey conducted by Dheeraj Sharma (IIM–A) for the purpose of this study on two national and one regional party contestants with a sample size of 385, which comprised 210 male and 175 female residents of Delhi, via mall intercept method.

9. Lynn, *Political Campaign Planning Manual* 28.

10. 'USA election 1992 campaign', https://en.wikipedia.org/wiki/ United_States_presidential_election,_1992.

11. 'Election Night Victory Speech Grant Park, Illinois', 4 November 2008, http://obamaspeeches.com/E11-Barack-Obama-Election-Night-Victory-Speech-Grant-Park-Illinois-November-4-2008.htm.

12. Ibid.

13. Singh, Neha, 'Was BJP CM Candidate Kiran Bedi Trying to Run Away from Interview with NDTV Anchor Ravish Kumar', IBTimes.co.in, 28 January 2015, http://www.ibtimes. co.in/was-bjp-cm-candidate-kiran-bedi-trying-run-away-interviewndtv-anchor-ravish-kumar-621734.

14. Williams, C.B., and Gulati, G., 'The Political Impact of Facebook: Evidence from the 2006 Midterm Elections and 2008 Nomination Contest', *Politics and Technology Review*, 2008.

15. Entman, R.M., 'Framing: Toward Clarification of a Fractured Paradigm', *Journal of Communication*, 1993, pp. 51-58.

16. Wheeldon, Johannes and McBrien, Alex, '(Mis)Representing the 2008 Prorogation: Agendas, Frames, and Debates in Canada's Mediacracy', *Canadian Journal of Communication* 39:3, 2014, pp. 307–309.

17. Unnithan, Chitra, '4Ps of Marketing Helped Modi Become Prime Minister: Study', *Times of India*, 30 May 2014, http:// timesofindia.indiatimes.com/india/4Ps-of-marketing-helped-Modi-become-Prime-Minister-Study/articleshow/35741339. cms.

18. 'BJP's Panna Pramukh Ensured That More Voters Step Out to Vote', *DNA*, 8 February 2015, http://www.dnaindia.com/ india/report-bjp-s-panna-pramukh-ensured-that-morevoters-step-out-to-vote-2059120.

A NOTE ON THE AUTHORS

Dheeraj Sharma is a professor and chairperson of marketing at the Indian Institute of Management, Ahmedabad (IIM-A). Sharma earned his doctoral degree with a major in marketing and a double minor in psychology and quantitative analysis from Louisiana Tech University, USA. He has taught and presented research papers at numerous education institutions in North America, Europe and Asia.

Sharma has authored over hundred papers and five books on marketing, consumer behaviour, B2B marketing management, cross-cultural research and leadership. He has four upcoming books on international business, sport marketing management, healthcare and talent management in India.

The co-author, Narayan Singh Rao, was a PGPX student at IIM-A. He is the founder and CEO of the start-up, The Indian Iris.